MOAN

ANONYMOUS ESSAYS ON FEMALE ORGASM

Collected by Emma Koenig

Foreword by Rachel Bloom

NEW YORK BOSTON

Grand Central Publishing
Hachette Book Group
1290 Avenue of the Americas, New York, NY 10104
grandcentralpublishing.com
twitter.com/grandcentralpub

First Edition: May 2018

Grand Central Publishing is a division of Hachette Book Group, Inc. The Grand Central Publishing name and logo is a trademark of Hachette Book Group, Inc.

The publisher is not responsible for websites (or their content) that are not owned by the publisher.

The Hachette Speakers Bureau provides a wide range of authors for speaking events. To find out more, go to www.hachettespeakersbureau.com or call (866) 376-6591.

Print book interior design by Abby Reilly.

Library of Congress Cataloging-in-Publication Data

Names: Koenig, Emma, compiler.
Title: Moan : essays on female orgasm / collected by Emma Koenig ; foreword by Rachel Bloom.
Description: First edition. | New York : Grand Central Publishing, [2018]
Identifiers: LCCN 2017025281| ISBN 9781455540556 (trade pbk.) | ISBN 9781478988366 (audio download) | ISBN 9781455540549 (ebook)
Subjects: LCSH: Female orgasm. | Women--Sexual behavior. | Sexual intercourse. | Sexual excitement.
Classification: LCC HQ29 .K64 2018 | DDC 306.7082--dc23
LC record available at https://lccn.loc.gov/2017025281

ISBNs: 978-1-4555-4055-6 (trade paperback), 978-1-4789-8836-6 (audio download), 978-1-4555-4054-9 (ebook)

Printed in the United States of America

LSC-C

10 9 8 7 6 5 4 3 2 1

For you, and your next orgasm.

Contents

Foreword

Hello. My name is Rachel Bloom. And, like half of you out there on planet Earth, I am the owner of a clitoris. Specifically, a 1987 clitoris sedan with four-wheel drive, 0 percent APR, and a pinkish-tan hood.

We clitoris owners can sometimes get a raw deal. (Side note: Raw Deal is also what I call my clitoris after a night of lovemaking.) The clitoris can be an enigma not only to those who approach it, but sometimes to those who own it. It took me almost twenty years of masturbating to kind of understand what brings me to orgasm. I say "kind of" because, even now, I am still surprised by my clitoris's own abilities and shortcomings. Or sometimes longcomings. Like, it's been seven seconds and I'm still coming? Impressive, my little raw deal.

First, I am glad that this book exists for those *without* clitorises. (I will henceforth refer to those people as "men" to talk about my own sexual experiences, though I acknowledge that many of you out there have many other different types of partners.)

When I was little, my mother warned me that "most men won't care about" my pleasure. However, I have pleasantly found the opposite to be true. Most of the men I've been with have been eager to please and super open to doing whatever it takes to get me off. When I tell them exactly what I want, they're not threatened; rather, they are relieved, jubilant, and then super turned on (in that order).

For this reason, I have never faked an orgasm. Never. Not once. I know what I want because I've been giving myself orgasms since age eleven and, as a result, was making myself come for about seven years before I let any penis-owner put his grimy man hands down there. The way I learned how to masturbate was very scholarly: I read a lot of puberty books. These books not only told me how to masturbate but also told me that most women can come only from clitoral stimulation.

Yet I am still insecure about not having an orgasm the "right" way. Even with all the puberty books, even with all the *Savage Lovecast*s, I am still insecure about my own clitoral orgasm. I pine for the idea of a "pure orgasm," aka coming from just a penis inside me.

A big part of this insecurity comes from hearing other women brag about their own vaginal orgasms. I remember confiding to one of my bragging friends that I couldn't come from sex alone, and she looked at me condescendingly and said that I just "hadn't been in love enough yet." When women I knew discussed sex and didn't bring up having a vaginal orgasm, they still glossed over the part involving any sort of clitoral stimulation as if it were a shameful thing. Once again, I relied on books and magazine articles to tell me that it was okay and normal to touch myself during sex.

Despite all the cliterature I read, I was still insecure about my orgasms. What if all that masturbating from such a young age had gotten me into a habit I couldn't break? Maybe if I'd masturbated less I would have been less used to my own fingers and a penis alone would be able to make me come. 'Cause honestly, having an orgasm during sex can sometimes be a pain in the ass. Sometimes my clit is weirdly numb from the rigors of intercourse, sometimes my own hands get tired, sometimes I forgot to USB charge my normal vibrator so I have to use my backup vibrator, which is fine but isn't as good.

This is why I'm glad this book exists for us clitoris-havers out there. No matter how proud you are of your clitoris and all the amazing things it does, there will almost always be confusion and questions around it. I am not half as insecure about my orgasms now, but there is still this lingering feeling that I and my raw deal aren't up to snuff.

The anonymous essays that Emma has curated prove that there is no right or wrong way for a woman to have an orgasm. Everyone's story is truly different. This book makes me more okay with a lot of things I've been insecure about throughout my life. It's okay that what brings me pleasure during intercourse is different from what brings me to orgasm. It's okay that, on occasion, I don't need to have an orgasm during sex, or, as one anonymous essay writer puts it, "It's just not going to happen tonight."

I could go on and on about the reasons this book is important right now, but Emma goes over all those reasons in her introduction way better than I ever could, so I'll just say this: we're all just flesh monsters who shit, sleep, and fuck, so life's too short to not get the exact pleasure you want.

MOAN

Foreplay

Before I ever had my first kiss, I went to second base. Well, kind of. The tamest possible version of second base. I was twelve years old; pre–bat mitzvah but post–crossing the threshold of menstruation and leg shaving. It was a time when I was strangely confident. Of course, I wasn't immune to insecurities. I mean, I was one of the tallest girls in my grade, I had the hair of Michael J. Fox—as Teen Wolf—and a mustache. (All of this is still true except for my height—this was about the time I stopped growing.) And I'd experienced my fair share of mean girls, unrequited crushes, cruel teasing, embarrassing AOL conversations, being the least athletic person in the history of sports, continually telling my parents and believing that "Today is the worst day of my life!," etc. But to be twelve, at least in the year 2000, at least for me, was to exist in this golden era before you were *fully* indoctrinated with society's master plan: to make women feel bad about themselves and how they look. How else are they going to get you to spend that much on cream for cellulite?!

I was in a basement in New Jersey, watching *The Rocky Horror Picture Show*. This setting may sound like the beginning of a horror movie to you, but I promise the story doesn't end with me waking up missing a kidney. (Or does it? Stay tuned!) Anyway, a shaggy-haired boy from Hebrew school sat next to me, and halfway through the movie, under a blanket, he began to slowly feel me up over my black sports bra from Macy's. I can still remember how heightened it felt, even though he never actually touched my skin. In between each subtle movement, he would whisper, "Is this okay?" and I would nod. I was calm. I knew this person. It wasn't moving too fast. It felt right.

He asked if he could kiss me. I said no. I wasn't ready for that yet. Kissing seemed like it'd be more intimate and intense than someone touching a barely formed body part of mine through thick fabric, a body part I had almost no relationship with yet.

I should probably mention that there were other Hebrew school friends in the room at this time. Which made my decision to keep the experience pretty PG a lot easier. I think everyone I grew up with would say that many of their coming-of-age experiences happened around other people because you never get to be alone with someone when you're that young. So you must eschew modesty and make do!

I emerged from the basement feeling confused about certain plot points in *Rocky Horror* and conflicted about my over-the-sports-bra experience. I thought I had liked what was happening. It was exciting and fun to be touched in this way. And yet, it felt fairly ordinary—like things had unfolded exactly as they were supposed to. But I had no emotional or physical reference point for sexual experiences. So while it was easy to feel good *during* it, I wasn't sure how I was supposed to feel *after* it. When my mom picked me up that night, my face was red. It was as if my whole body was broadcasting that someone touched my boobs. Or "boobs." All of a sudden, I went from feeling in control of my destiny to feeling really guilty and uncomfortable.

I knew, even at twelve, that women are made to feel unnecessarily ashamed about sexual behavior. And I'd just had my first taste of that shame. I had to keep reminding myself I'd done nothing wrong. That night was a turning point for me. I decided that moving forward, I never, ever wanted to feel the slightest bit bad for wanting something so natural and normal. I declared myself a "sexual warrior."

I wasn't having sex yet. That was a while away. But even then, I knew that I had to leave breadcrumbs for my future self. If you felt bad at every checkpoint leading up to sex, wouldn't you feel bad about sex itself?

Thus, I tried to adopt an enlightened attitude about anything related to sex. I saw it as just one of the categories of being human. You eat, you sleep, you piss, you shit, you laugh, you cry, *you have sex*. It was an essential part of existence. I was a sexual person because...I was a person.

But the older I got, the more I came to realize that I couldn't live in a vacuum. I was not at the center of some free-love, no-judgment, Samantha Jones–meets-a-hippie-commune-meets-a-porno-directed-by-a-woman fantasy world that I so desired. (Yes, I've heard of Burning Man, but in *my* fantasy world, there's access to a shower and you don't have to bike in sand.)

And even if I fancied myself a sexual warrior, attempting to go out into the world with intellectual and emotional armor, I underestimated the world.

I underestimated the lifelong obstacle course I would have to navigate as a woman. The one all women must navigate. When I was twelve, I had already been told I couldn't wear a tank top at school because it was distracting to boys. Strange men were already sexually harassing me. But I didn't yet know of the misogynistic horrors that lay ahead. The things that would chip away at the optimism and confidence of my younger self.

But despite these unanticipated roadblocks, I attempted to continually refine my ideas about sexuality. I strove to be positive and curious and accepting, hoping to avoid feeling bad about being a sexual person, hoping to avoid feeling bad about being a person.

Many, many years after the adolescent second-base experience served as a catalyst to begin examining my ideas about sex, I was having sex with someone for the first time. And it wasn't going so well. The longer it went, the less turned on I became. But in my rose-colored-glasses view of sex, I tried to roll with it. *I strove to be positive and curious and accepting.*

And while I could've chalked this up to awkwardness or nerves or sexual incompatibility (all of which may've been factors), this time was different. Because when it was over, my partner told me I'd had an orgasm. He did not *ask* if I had, but confidently *told* me I had.

It was instant cognitive dissonance. I was being told something about myself that directly contradicted my reality. It's like if someone were to say, "You just ate an ice cream cone" after you'd brushed your teeth. You'd feel more than a little perplexed. I hadn't even gotten close to "Ooh, that feels kinda nice," let alone to "Holy shit! I didn't even know it was possible to feel that good!" but somehow this discrepancy wasn't apparent to my partner. I searched my mind for ANYTHING that could've been misinterpreted as an orgasm—did I make an orgasm-esque microexpression for 0.02 seconds?—but I couldn't think of a single moment that I'd projected even the slightest hint of ecstasy. So I gently explained that I hadn't come and gave some tips for things that might help in the future. I was optimistic.

But when the future arrived, weeks later, the sex was even worse. This time I was in such physical and emotional discomfort that I felt paralyzed. Like I didn't know how to stop it. To my surprise, I was unsure of how to speak up for myself. I wanted it to be over, but my brain couldn't send the message to my mouth. I realized that moans of pleasure, which I'd previously thought were a somewhat theatrical part of sex, were actually my involuntary reactions to feeling good. Because this time, I was completely silent.

And I felt like a vessel for someone else to use, rather than a person. It's a sensation that still upsets me to this day. It's something I never want to feel again.

I left in the morning with a smile on my face, but once I

was alone, I broke down in tears on the subway. I was confused as to how two people could have such wildly different perceptions of a shared experience, and guilty for not being able to advocate for myself, even though I'd felt safe enough to do so the previous time. I felt sad that I'd let myself suffer through a sexual experience I didn't want to be having. I kept asking myself why I couldn't speak up, and the only reason I could come up with was that I was so worried about hurting someone else's feelings that I severely neglected my own. *I wanted to be polite.* And that answer haunted me.

I parted ways from this person and was left with a lot of questions. How can there be such an ocean of distance between sexual partners? How could someone be so sure of a woman's orgasm with little effort to induce one and little evidence of its existence? Why does it sometimes feel like the hardest person to talk to about sex is the person you're having sex with? My thoughts wandered as I tried to dissect how things had unfolded and why.

Every remotely negative sexual memory came to the forefront of my mind—moments I hadn't thought about in years, details I had trained myself to be okay with. In an attempt to have a blanket positive outlook on sex, maybe I had avoided fully dealing with the moments when I was uncomfortable.

But it wasn't just the upsetting memories that rose to the surface. The joyful, positive, sexy AF occasions came to mind as well. What did *those* experiences have in common? What could I learn from them?

I thought about the conversations I'd had with my female

friends about the complications of sex. The times we'd assured our partners it was fine if we didn't come. The times we didn't want to give pointers to people we seriously liked, for fear of emasculating them, coming off as too aggressive, or screwing up the relationship. How even when we *did* feel comfortable providing instruction, we sometimes struggled to articulate exactly what we meant, particularly in the moment. How many times someone had used too much force (did someone start a misguided rumor that clits are made of steel?), ignoring our insistence that it just wasn't going to happen that night. The people we dated who were happy to get blowjobs, but hardly ever went down on us. The relationships, both casual and long term, during which we never had orgasms. I knew the immense frustration and heartache this had caused not just my friends, but their partners as well.

I thought about the men who'd bragged to me about how quickly they'd made women come.

"But how did you know she came?" I would always inquire.

"Because she dug her fingernails into my back," said one.

"Because her legs were shaking," said another.

"Because she was moaning."

"Because I just knew."

Partners, I regret to inform you that fingernails in the back is not irrefutable evidence of an orgasm. Again, who is spreading these rumors? Let me also say, as a straightish person, that I don't think the female orgasm dilemma is an exclusively heterosexual problem at all, but I suspect there's a higher instance of philosophical disconnect between men and women.

Which raises the question: how do men and women even learn about the female orgasm? We are raised in a culture that both shames and demands sexuality. If sex ed is even offered at our schools, it tends to be limited and unrealistic (and typically from a heterosexual-only point of view). We are most often learning about female orgasm from movies (where it's fake), pornography (where it's fake), and real life (where it can still be fake!).

So, I wanted to get to the truth. I wanted to create something where women got to share all the things they wanted to say about orgasm and sex and dating, but could not—the things that are difficult to articulate to a partner or even a trusted friend. I wanted to delve into the real experience of female orgasm and start a dialogue about how women achieve sexual pleasure, something that, even today, is often ignored, devalued, or misunderstood. I wanted to display the spectrum of desire. I wanted to talk about it all, the painful and the beautiful. I wanted to do this not only because female orgasm can sometimes be challenging to achieve and/or talk about, but also because I suspect that when we talk about female orgasm, something deeper is at play. When we misunderstand or ignore female orgasm, we are misunderstanding and ignoring women.

So I drafted an email asking women to anonymously contribute their experiences about orgasm. One possible prompt was to write an essay entitled "How to Make Me Come" and imagine that you could give it to a past, present, or future sexual partner. What would you want them to know, free of judgment or repercussion? But mostly, I just wanted people to talk about female orgasm and sex, in whatever way made sense to them.

I reached out to some friends. They reached out to some friends. They reached out to some friends...and I slowly began to build a collective of women who had something to say. People responded immediately with intense affirmation and stories of their own. I basked in the rush I got from seeing people opening up. It confirmed that this is something a lot of women are itching to talk about. And as people began to write pieces, and I had the privilege of being the first to read them, I could feel this expansion of self. Something catalyzed by a bad experience had grown into a celebration of women's ideas and feelings.

This started as an internet project in August 2015 and has evolved into this very book! One that I'm so psyched you purchased and are reading at this very moment. (Oh, you didn't buy it yet? You're standing in the bookstore, looking at this, debating whether or not to buy it? Well...this may sound weird, but I'm suddenly having a premonition about your future. I think you are destined to buy this book! No pressure, though.)

On a basic level, I just want people to feel good. Everyone deserves to feel good.

But it goes beyond that. All of our sex lives are shaped by culture and political views. You cannot talk about how women are perceived and treated by society without talking about how society perceives and treats female sexuality. We are inextricably linked to our sexuality because, as I keep repeating, at the risk of already annoying you, to be a sexual person is to be a person! So if the world treats *your sexuality* like it's fucked up or not real, is it any surprise that the world also treats *you* like *you're* fucked up or not real, even in areas that have nothing to do with sex?

There is no shortage of material related to orgasm, online and off. And it seems like almost every magazine or website related to women in any way talks about orgasm at some point. While I think there is definitely value in a brief, salient article, a video, or an infographic, they're not showing you the whole picture. I, for one, will never forget reading in *Cosmo* that you should dip a guy's balls in a carbonated beverage. Oddly enough, that has never come up in my sex life. Yet!

Learning about sex from a buzzy tips list is like trying to learn an entire language by looking at the top ten helpful phrases. While it's super useful to know how to order a coffee and ask for directions, it doesn't mean you would be equipped to carry on a conversation with a native speaker. To be able to do that, you have to immerse yourself. Hopefully this book can be like studying abroad, a chance to immerse yourself in the stories of female sexuality. And afterward, you may find it easier to "speak the language" than before.

Like *clit*, *cunt*, or *vagina*, *feminism* is still seen by many as a dirty word. On average, women continue to earn considerably less than men. Access to safe, legal abortions is not a given. Some people even think women should be punished for getting abortions. More than three million girls are at risk for female genital mutilation annually. Every nine seconds in the United States, a woman is assaulted or beaten. Each day, three or more women are killed by their boyfriends or husbands. LGBT women face the greatest risk of discrimination and homicidal violence. The risk increases for LGBT women of color. DONALD TRUMP, WHO HAS BRAGGED ABOUT SEXUALLY ASSAULTING WOMEN, WAS ELECTED PRESIDENT OF THE UNITED STATES. I could go on and on. I could keep citing the devastating facts and statistics that impact women and girls. But I just want you to know (and I hope you already do, but I say this because many people, both men and women, do not understand or acknowledge this truth) that across the world, women are still treated like shit.

So why am I bringing up all these serious issues facing us when I'm talking about orgasms, which may seem frivolous by comparison? Because all these issues are linked to how women are perceived and treated, on micro and macro levels. Paying attention to female orgasm means acknowledging that women are full people, deserving of experiencing pleasure. Maybe if we focus on caring for a woman's clit, it might make it more obvious that we should also care for her heart and her brain. And if we feel empowered to speak up in our bedrooms, we can feel inspired to continue to voice our opinions on cultural and political stages.

Because talking about such an important, emotional issue as sex can be exposing, I chose not to add any more details about the authors than those they'd written themselves in the bodies of their essays. Some of the writers would have been happy to put their names on their work, and while I didn't want to force anonymity on anyone, it made the most sense that if one should be anonymous, then everyone should. If I were to tell you up front how old everyone is, what their sexual orientation is, what their race and ethnicity is, what their job is, where they grew up, where they live now, what their first name is, those facts would inevitably inform your experience of reading the piece.

And the goal here is to foster open-mindedness not only in the contributors, who have the opportunity to write, knowing that their identities will be protected, but also for readers, who I hope can feel a specific sort of empathy and compassion reading these pieces—where you aren't caught up in the biographical details of a person, potentially distorting their truth.

So why am *I* not anonymous? When I first created this project for the internet, I remained anonymous for many reasons, but the two most important ones were: First, I didn't want the identity of the creator to get in the way of the project. This project was my idea and my passion, but it isn't about me. In fact, I have an essay of my own in this book and I want it to live as part of a collection of voices. When this launched, I felt it'd be a disservice to have people's judgments and perceptions about me get in the way of their feelings about the project. If someone might not like me (or whatever conclusion they drew about me based on Google results) but could actually really connect to the writing, I wanted to allow them the space to do that—this is kind of my version of *The Voice*. Second, I have been a woman on the internet for a while, and a woman for even longer! I know how it goes. And while I think I've gotten a lot better at coping with the truly disgusting, insulting, and sometimes scary comments that happen in reaction to opening your mouth while female online, it still fucking sucks. Like, you ever have one of those days where you don't want men to threaten to rape and kill you? Really? Me too! Wow, we have so much in common!

But since the project has gotten a chance to live and breathe in full anonymity since 2015, I now feel comfortable putting my name on it. Because, hey, it's something I created that I'm proud of. And after allowing the project to grow without having my identity overpower the narrative, I now want to shout from the rooftops that this baby is mine because it means so much to me. Also, my anxiety level about keeping this secret has been sky-high. Kudos to Banksy—I don't know how you do it!

In an ideal world, this book would be ten million pages long, and include the experiences and voices of every woman on the planet. But as you can see, this volume is just the tip of the iceberg. This is not the definitive book on female orgasm and sexuality, but rather an offering of an addition to the conversation. Just like with any attempt at giving pleasure, I have tried to be aware of how you might feel, what would feel good to you, and I have done my best to make you happy. But despite my best efforts, my methods might not work on everybody.

And here I am in this book extolling the female orgasm, but I want to acknowledge that there is a great deal of difficulty and pressure tied up in orgasms, too. If you can't come, whether it's one time or every time, it's COMPLETELY okay. That doesn't make you less of a woman or less of a sexual being. I use the female orgasm as the touchstone, but really, an orgasm is less about that one moment and more about everything that leads up to it.

This book is not a guide and it isn't a directive that says every woman must come and every partner must make a woman come. It's more like, hey, pay attention to female pleasure . . . Pay attention to women.

When I was twelve in that basement, as *Rocky Horror* began to play, I watched those iconic disembodied red lips sing what would be the prologue of the first time I dipped my toes in sexual waters, and I didn't know who the voice belonged to.

As an adult, I have put together this collection of anonymous voices singing their stories. I hope it will serve as a sort of prologue for your own future sexual adventures and conversations.

HARDER

"I started equating having an orgasm with just getting really, really close to it."

I've only come once in my entire life, and even that feels like a fluke.

I had arrived a long time ago at the sexual conclusion that dudes came and I was mostly along for the ride. Like, *sure*, I totally came. I'm tired and hot and I can hear the blood rushing in my ears and am probably bathed in some dewy, womanly glow; roll off me and wash your hands so I can go get a glass of water and some pretzel chips. I don't think I ever actually thought my own pure pleasure was an option. I don't think I really even knew what my own pure pleasure felt like. After a while, I started equating having an orgasm with just getting really, really close to it. I didn't understand the burst of euphoria everyone was always talking about. When I was crabby and people told me I needed to get laid, my response was "I get laid all the time and I'm still in a bad mood." I just didn't get it.

My single climactic experience still seems like a dream, so far removed from my immediate catalog of experiences that I can't tell at times if I made it up or just serendipitously tapped into a part of my body I'll never access again. It was with my boyfriend at the time: a thoughtful and sweet but truly and hopelessly misguided creative guy whose idea of romance was an Edible Arrangement and relentlessly trying to dry-hump me while we watched a movie on the couch. I'd lowered my sexual expectations with him to at least making it to work on time if he decided to get frisky in the morning and definitely getting laid anytime he went out drinking with his coworkers.

But on a tremendous, rare night when surely pigs flew, Halley's comet shot by, and volcanoes spouted ice cubes elsewhere in the world, we got intimate and I finally came. It wasn't the monumental experience of the movies where the woman is crawling up the walls rapturously or shouting to the heavens, hair mussed and cheeks tear-stained. I was into it, of course, and everything felt great, and then it was just as if his penis flipped on a switch in a room I'd never entered. My whole body was surfing on a wave of pure bliss. Immediately after, I was the most *chill* I'd ever been. The house could have been burning down around me but I couldn't be bothered to care. I looked at him lounging in the crook of my arm and remarked, "I feel really good. I just feel really great!" Maybe it was the peppy lilt of my voice, but he could definitely tell something was different from our usual postcoital conversation.

"Is this the first time I've ever made you come?" he asked, almost accusingly.

"Ummm... no, I mean, umm..." The jig was up. He could tell I'd massaged the truth about my side of our sexual interactions all those other times. He was visibly annoyed, but kissed me nonetheless and went back to his normal tradition of almost shamefully peeling off the condom and washing his hands in the bathroom with the door closed.

After that, I never got anywhere close to that feeling again. I continued to have sex with him for about six months, until I very quickly fell out of love with him and our emotionally unhealthy relationship. I moved on from it and have since had sex with plenty of other men, who all collectively assumed they were the best in bed, but I still couldn't find that perfect moment, that bloom of ecstasy I knew so fleetingly. I even fucked on molly once, thinking that would surely get me to the mountaintop, and I still didn't come.

Upon a recommendation from a friend and personal rewatching of the entire *Sex and the City* series, I finally invested in a vibrator. It was the nicest "back massager" they carried at Brookstone, hot pink and packaged in a black velvet box. I soon realized that, having never truly explored my own sexual wants and interests, having always let them take a back seat to the men on top of me, I didn't know how to get myself off. I had experimented a little in college (as everyone is wont to do, I guess) with watching porn and using my hand, but nothing seemed to work as well as another human body. I put the vibrator in my bedside table drawer and there it stayed.

Once, I had taken home a guy I regularly hooked up with and he woke me up the next morning with his hands on my tits. We had the most lackluster sex and he came almost immediately. He then put all his clothes on, saying he needed to get to a pickup basketball game with his friends, and left me all hot and bothered at eight thirty a.m. I furiously grabbed my vibrator and quickly felt hopeless. The low buzz sounded like taunting. I put it away and just lay there until I had to get up and shower. I'm sure that guy played basketball better than ever that morning, shooting hoops with the ease and agility of a man lighter, more satisfied, and happier than usual.

In a world where men can come from the right breeze hitting them while they stretch, and female celebrities publicly talk about the need to orgasm, I felt sadly left out of the conversation. My journey prompted me to learn to understand my body in ways I'd previously disregarded, and I've become more ready to demand that my own needs be met. Halley's comet isn't coming back until 2061, and I'm ready to get my light switched a few more times before then.

"Accept that you are not Jennifer Lawrence and let yourself feel good."

How to come during sex

It should be noted that this unfortunately is a guide for straight couples, as that is my only reference, but I hope some of it applies to gay sex as well.

For the women:

1. **Masturbate. Masturbate. Masturbate.** Pay attention to what feels good and how you got there. If rubbing your clit hard and fast is how you get it done, guess what? That's what needs to get done in the bedroom.
2. **Stop performing.** I have faked more orgasms than I can even count. This is because I was just performing for my partner because I wanted him to come faster for whatever reason and I knew he wouldn't unless he thought I was enjoying myself. That's on me. Maybe if I weren't faking it,

he actually would have tried something else that I would've liked.

3. **Make your voice heard.** Just say what feels good or lead him in the direction of what feels good. If you really feel like you don't like to talk, guide him physically. Maybe even play with yourself a little to give him an idea of how you do it so he can replicate that. Most guys are into watching a girl touch herself. He gets a show/instructional visual and you actually get wet. It's a win-win.
4. **Love or at least like yourself.** This is the hardest. Thankfully the mood has shifted a little and the world is showing us real women in entertainment and advertising, but it is still ingrained in all of us that if we don't look a certain way we are not sexy or fuckable. If you are too nervous about how you look during sex, you are never going to come. We all look DUMB AS FUCK when we come. We scrunch up our faces, make weird noises or don't make noise at all, and feel out of control and therefore weird, and it does not look like Jennifer Lopez sexy-moaning in *The Boy Next Door*. It looks stupid and is extremely vulnerable. If you are judging yourself from inside the sex, it is not gonna happen. Accept that you are not Jennifer Lawrence and let yourself feel good.
5. **Wait.** If you find you are too in your head and wrapped up in how your partner is doing, wait until he comes and then reward yourself. I have found that feeling a man come in me fills me with such

relief and satisfaction that I am almost immediately able to grind my way to orgasm. Guys normally stay hard for a bit and now that you know he's good, take that opportunity to make sure you are good as well. If he is too sensitive after coming for you to ride it out, let him know you didn't come and if he is worth ANYTHING he will manually help you out.

"I've had amazing sex with one-night stands and horrible sex with a longtime boyfriend."

As a former dancer, I've always been very in tune with my body. In order to be pleasured, I know exactly how each part needs to be touched. I can come by myself without a vibrator or any *Magic Mike XXL* pictures. I close my eyes, engage my lower abdominals, and when I've worked myself up, I envision the color red. Sounds strange, but envisioning a color helps clear the mind of all intruding thoughts. All of a sudden, I feel that burst, a wonderful release of tension that pulsates up toward my heart. I am elated, breathless, and with a fresh, lighter gait, ready to tackle the rest of my day. Some people enjoy a midday nap, but I find a late-afternoon masturbation session can cure most frustrations.

When it comes to sex, it's very much a case-by-case basis of what works and what doesn't, which is why this topic is so damn complicated. I've had amazing sex with one-night stands and horrible sex with a longtime boyfriend. My pleasure is based on how comfortable I feel with the other person, and the ability of the man I'm with to make me feel wanted. This doesn't always match up with how long I've known the person.

There are a few trigger moves that take me from being kind of turned on to screaming, "Get inside of me right now!" First, alcohol. I don't mean getting shitfaced. I mean I love a glass or two of wine, which almost instantly puts me in a more relaxed and less inhibited mind space. Second, kissing my neck, right on the nape. Warm me up with a few light touches on my collarbone, a little tongue on the ear, and I'm halfway there. Seriously. The bristle of your beard against my cheek…I'm wet just thinking about it.

Like anyone on this planet, I have my own body insecurities. I sweat the fact that I have super-small, you-almost-can't-even-tell-they're-there boobs. Okay, I have no boobs. But the little mounds I do have yearn to be touched. Many of my friends complain that guys spend way too much time playing with their tits, like children with shiny new toys, but when a man reaches for my chest and seems to really get off on what it has to offer, in my mind, I feel as voluptuous and sexy as a Victoria's Secret angel. When a man retracts his hand as if he got lost in the dark and couldn't find what are supposed to be boobs on my chest, I have to try very hard to not withdraw in shame. Internally, I pump myself back up, reminding myself that I'm attractive and that he's lucky to be getting so intimate with me. But my brain is already wandering. I'm not totally "in it" anymore. I wish for a man to adore every inch of my body. What warm-blooded human wouldn't want that from a sexual partner? Sensing a person's extreme appreciation and adoration of your body is a huge turn-on.

So where were we…Ah, yes. We've wined and dined,

you've made the first move to kiss me (don't ask permission—just do it), and if your lips found their way to my neck, you're probably now naked in my bed. Throw it down. This is a direct order: throw me down. As I'm a petite li'l thang, men are sometimes afraid that they'll break me if they get too rough, but I don't break. Take control and use some force. I might steal the reins from you, and if you fight to steal them back, the reward is handsome.

Oral is fun. I love a guy who loves to give head. Enthusiasm to go to town on my snatch is fascinating, but for me, it's just foreplay. I come from the grind of sex. Apparently this is rare, and reason 1,379 why I hate condoms, but if we've just met, you're baggin' it up, bro. And because this is how I get off, I definitely enjoy a man who's packing large. But if you're not, there are alternatives. Two fingers work great!

All physical parts of sex can be switched up and adjusted for success, but if I'm not mentally in it, I'm not going to orgasm. I'll close my eyes, moan, and say, "I want you to come so hard" so you will, and it will be over. I only do this when I know it's not going to happen, in which case there could be a zillion reasons that have nothing to do with you, or one that might. Maybe I'm not that into you, or you're someone who I already know isn't that into me. This doesn't mean I need us to want to marry each other, but it helps when there's more than the fact that you were the only other single person left at the party. Not judging. We've all been there.

Sometimes attraction is purely sexual; we can ravage

each other and have no chance of being in a serious relationship. Sometimes the opposite is true. I may think you're an awesome human being but recoil at the idea of being naked with you. Why it's so hard to have both of these things from the same person, I don't think we'll ever know. But if we're on the same page, let's finish our drinks. Lightly clutch my neck with your hand, and pull my face toward yours for a kiss with enough pressure against my lips that I feel passion. Take a slight pause to stare into my eyes so the rest of the world melts away. Oh yeah, I'll come.

"Had I been molested, maybe? I would be asked this by more than one doctor, in a tone approaching hopefulness."

I wasn't sure if I could write this essay, seeing as my issue isn't about phantom orgasms. See, my problem is more that I haven't ever learned the trick to delaying climax whenever I feel like it. I've never *not* come.

Poor me, right? I'm pretty much the incarnation of everything frustrating about the stereotypes perpetuated by the porn industry. I come compulsively, loudly, and without any thought into the matter whatsoever. Whenever I mention this, however, people regard me as either a liar or some kind of mythical sex unicorn (which explains why I was always so popular with the virgin crowd).

But I exist. And to quote that Five for Fighting song about an irritatingly emo Superman: "It's not easy . . . to be . . . me."

But imagine that your memories of childhood are predominated not by events or pictures or thoughts but by physical sensations: discomfort, frustration, and a shame so deep it made you physically sick to your stomach. And above all of them, there's another feeling, one of simultaneous excitement and immediate relaxation. And that those three overwhelming negative physical sensations were mitigated only by that good feeling, which in return fed back into the bad ones; an endless, compulsive loop that made you feel out of control every time you wore tight pants to school, or had to pee during a long car ride, or found yourself wide awake after lights out, worrying about what life was like on the other side of your haftarah portion. In a sense, my entire life has been one long orgasm as distraction.

Whenever I was bored as a kid—and I mean, a REALLY little kid; my mom says I was doing it before I could crawl or express myself with something like "I'd prefer hentai to this *Bambi* shit, thanks"—I would rub my knuckle into the fabric covering my crotch. The thicker the better: mere underwear would have me reaching for the nearest stuffed animal to hump like a Care Bear molester. I usually came within forty-two seconds, something I once was able to time by seeing if I could get it in before the end of the Indigo Girls' cover of "Uncle John's Band," once they got to the final acoustic chorus: "Come on along or go alone, they've come to take the children home." (Why didn't my parents just give me a tape of the actual Grateful Dead instead of "modern" covers by Elvis Costello? That, I can't answer.)

As you can imagine, I didn't have very many friends during my early years. It was hard to find my social footing when I was constantly being pulled out of class and sent to the principal's office for "touching myself": an antiseptically vague euphemism used by public school administrators that roughly translates to "We don't want a lawsuit so we'll never tell you exactly why we're pissed at you."

The phrase remains such a deep-rooted trigger that well-meaning guys have found themselves literally kicked out of my bed for asking if they could watch. Looking back, I can see the tough spot I put everyone in: upsetting the kids and faculty alike, who thought they were witnessing some sort of sweaty epileptic seizure four or five times a class.

Unfortunately, social pariah + lack of friends = a very bored little girl with an overactive imagination and a lot of free time waiting in the car while my mom begged to not have me expelled or sent to a "special" school for the pre-pubescently perverse. Bored, uncomfortable, and with a lot of time on my hands. And as far as I could figure, my hands were good for just about one thing.

I didn't masturbate all the time in public (and in private, though the latter was naturally not as much of an issue) because I was some kind of deviant. It was just the only thing that reliably made me feel good. I was prone to constant (yet unrelated!) urinary tract infections as a kid, and getting myself off—that quick buildup while thinking about Jeff Goldblum in *Jurassic Park*, a POPPING kind of release, followed by an immediate desire to do it all again—was the only way to escape the feelings of shame, anxiety, and physical discomfort that far predated my first actual memory.*

---

* Which, luckily (?), isn't about a time I was caught masturbating but the time I shoved my friend Alex down three flights of steps at the Bronx Zoo (we were pushing our strollers ahead of us in a race to the top and he was winning), knocking out his two front teeth and forever fucking up his nose. My first memory: anger, blood, tears, and the thrill of my very first ambulance ride, as my guilty histrionics confused the EMTs who arrived that I was the injured party.

I feel bad for my parents, who didn't want me to have any hang-ups about sexual identity but were caught between progressive parenting and firm boundaries. They would talk to me like an adult who could logically comprehend the concept of "an appropriate time and place." Help didn't come from teachers, who worried about overstepping or being accused of something terrible; nor did I find comfort from therapists who pried and probed to shape this very (to me) physical issue into something more significant and disturbing that could be explained by the *DSM*. Had I been molested, maybe? I would be asked this by more than one doctor, in a tone approaching hopefulness. No. The only person who touched me was myself. If I had associated "being touched down there" with being forced and out of my own control, maybe that would have fit. But the bum fact of it was that masturbation was the only way I could take back control; something to soothe myself in a world that felt so tightly constricted.

My motto has always been "Why mess with a good thing?" and that applies as much to getting off as it did to the rattail I rocked from first grade to junior year. I never really changed up my technique (though, thank God, by high school I did learn to ask for a bathroom pass instead of diddling discreetly under the table in the middle of pre-calc). This is all to say, the first time I had sex—in college, consensually, with a sweet trombonist, at 4:20 on Yom Kippur—it was completely game-changing. "You mean if I put something UP INSIDE ME, it could feel good in a TOTALLY DIFFERENT way WHILE feeling good in the SAME WAY??? Sometimes AT THE SAME TIME???" Consider my mind (and that considerate dude) blown.

They say that most women don't come the first time they have sex. I had already come twice during the buildup and then a couple (like three or four) times more during the act itself, so I guess I had half a dozen reasons to count myself #blessed. Although considering all the fucked-up shit I associated with sexuality at that point, it felt less like a blessing and more like me finally putting my particular set of skills to good use.

Overnight (and into the next morning) I discovered that the reason people call masturbation "pleasuring oneself" was because orgasms were supposed to be *pleasant*. Not just "the only thing that doesn't feel completely awful, but still makes you feel totally disgusting afterward." Like, it felt fun. And funny! I kept laughing every time I got off, because for once someone was looking at me with something other than sheer horror and/or confusion bordering on nausea. Instead, I found that guys were THRILLED when I offered up, unsolicited, a running tally of how many times I was getting off. They looked at me with something approaching grateful lust: I was making THEM feel like sexual studs because I was just doing what I did naturally! HOME RUN! By the time fall break rolled around, I was the world's happiest empowered come-slut.

Sometimes I honestly felt bad for the guys, since they seemed to have to concentrate so very hard and for a pretty long time just to get off even once. It seemed to really tire them out too, which also made me pity them because my entire life I'd been able to use coming like a hard reset on a crashed browser: I functioned faster and more efficiently after clearing my sexual cache. A nap seemed a little redundant after a good fuck.

They say that masturbating too much can ruin sex, but I found, little by little, the opposite to be true. It was hard to go back to the frustrating friction of rubbing myself when I knew that I could just as easily find a guy more than happy to be used to scratch that itch. I guess you could say that I was slutty, but it was more like I was lazy and disassociated. I had a hard time seeing why sex was that big of a deal, or why I couldn't have it with more than one person just because I was in a relationship, which was OBVIOUSLY its own separate thing. Being someone's girlfriend always felt like the transactional part: getting meals and free shit in exchange for my time, attention, and emotional energy, far scarcer (and therefore more valuable) resources than a mutually beneficial, (relatively) brief stress-relieving exercise.

Now that I'm older, my tastes have changed once again. Sex, with all its complications, personal preference, and ego-soothing ("It's all right, baby, it happens to everyone" is something I say with my fingers crossed, since performance anxiety is antithetical to the way I'm hardwired) can be all the things I used to climax AWAY from. It can be stressful. It can be uncomfortable. It can lead to painful urinary tract infections. And worst of all (in my limited and obviously privileged experience), it can be mind-numbingly BORING. Even if I come—and I still always do, though after three decades, the novelty of orgasming has worn pretty thin—it's not always a release. Sometimes I find myself more agitated after sex than I was before it, and I find myself resenting the men who, sated on the mistaken belief that my pleasure was something they gave to me instead of something I took from them, will sleepily inquire after how many times they made me come.

I'm not a monster, nor do I think my orgasm has much to do with gender politics (seeing as how I grasped my crotch long before I was aware of the concept of patriarchy), so I try not to be an asshole during postcoital recapping. But I bristle at the idea that my own pleasure needs to be quantifiable in a way that my partner's doesn't. Nor am I always keeping count: the one upside about being chronically overstimulated is that there's never been any point in keeping count.

So, when asked if I came, how hard, or how many times, I will usually respond with a sly smile and a word thrown over my shoulder as I turn back to a book; to the bathroom; to the computer; out into the night.

"Guess."

"I feel her strap-on bulging through her pants and boxer briefs."

"I'll see you inside, babe, enjoy your cancer stick."

"Yeah, yeah, yeah." I roll my eyes and toss her my keys. She catches them easily and unlocks my door, already knowing which key is the right one. I cross the street to buy my nightly loosie from the bodega, and feel proud I have waited through a whole night of drinking to smoke. As I wait to catch the bodega man's eye, I feel light and crack a smile at the kids fighting over which candy to buy with their coins. With a nod I exchange my fifty cents for a single cigarette. I light it from the tethered, scotch-taped lighter at the counter and leave. Settling in on my stoop, I let my mind wander to her. I review our night out dancing, her hand on the back of my neck, her sweaty forehead pressed up against mine as she leans down to kiss me. I love her big hands on my waist and how small she makes me feel. I start to feel myself get wet and shake my head at my endless attraction to her. With a sigh, I stomp out my cigarette and head upstairs. I intend to leave my sexual thoughts outside, promising myself to let her sleep. She has a big workday ahead, and I do not want to be the reason for it not to go well.

I open the door, surprised to find all the lights out.

"Honey? Don't you dare jump out and scare me. Really, I mean—"

"I'm in here!"

I leave my coat, bag, and keys in a familiar lump on the floor and find her waiting in my bedroom, already comfortably settled into a book. She sheepishly smiles at me and pats the bed next to her.

"Come sit with me for a bit before you get ready for bed," she says. I hesitate, thinking about my sweaty, gross clothes and unwashed face. "Please?"

I admire her lean, strong body and oblige. She turns on her side toward me as I lie down beside her, on my back. I am restless, wishing to begin my nightly pre-bed routine. Her hand rests comfortably on my stomach, and she begins to kiss me. As we kiss, my mind wanders. Her kisses are so perfect, just the right amount of pressure, her strong tongue pressing against mine, was the cable bill due today? Or was that tomorrow? Ugh and tomorrow I have to go all the way to Queens to pick up that paperwork... Focus, focus. I acknowledge my distractions, and try to focus on her kisses, feeling only a slight tinge of guilt.

She pauses to climb on top of me.

"Baaaabe, let me wash up first, yeah?"

"Nuh-uh. You're not going anywhere." She leans in close to my ear and whispers, "You're not going anywhere until I make you come for me."

I smile and give in to her game. Looming above me, she starts to kiss me again. As she lowers herself down, I feel her strap-on bulging through her pants and boxer briefs. I immediately get wet, surprised and excited that she has been waiting for me with the dick on. I moan with satisfaction as she presses herself against me and squirm with excitement.

When she is fucking me, my mind is overwhelmed with pleasure. She is rough tonight, not letting me touch her, moving me around the bed however she likes. My moans tell her that I like it. She knows how much it turns me on to give over control, to submit and let her have her way. I love pleasing her. She fucks me hard and talks dirty to me, calling me a bad girl but never a bitch. She knows exactly how to occupy this dominant role without offending me, she knows my boundaries and respects them. She fucks me from behind, turning me over and slapping my ass several times, so that it stings. She pulls my hair, bringing my head back toward hers.

"Are you going to let me come inside you tonight?"

I nod my head yes and try to kiss her, but she won't allow it. She flips me over and we switch positions, so that she is back on top of me. She begins thrusting, fucking me slow and steady. I feel the dick slide in and out of me. She pauses sometimes, making me press my hips up toward hers to have it fully inside me again. I grab the bottom of her harness, just below her ass, and push her deeper inside me. She starts to moan and I know she is going to come soon. Her clit rubs against mine, and we press and grind our bodies together. I feel waves of my approaching orgasm course through my body and clench my muscles to encourage it.

"You ready? Are you going to come for me? Yeah?"

"Yes, please don't stop, yes."

We both come together in a release of moans, sweat, hands pushing and grabbing, mouths open and breathing heavily. I collapse on my back, a smile on my face. I push the lube bottle onto the floor and it lands with a thud that makes her jump. I pat her chest twice.

"Good job, babe. That was incredible and hot. So fucking hot."

"Yeah, you like it like that, don't you?"

"Shhhhh."

I giggle and give her shoulder a shove. I'm embarrassed at the raunchy nature of our sex and how intensely I like it. I know she likes fucking me rough and hard, and wonder why she will only do it when she's drunk. Maybe she's embarrassed, too? I look over at her satisfied face, and feel proud that I made her come from fucking. No vibrators needed.

"When you make me come, I don't want to be reminded about how for so long I was saving myself for marriage."

Don't talk about Jesus. It should seem like a given, but what if I told you that from the ages of sixteen to twenty-three all I talked about was Jesus? I guess that's what a born-again Christian does, but it still feels like a fever dream when I think about the fact that I was essentially saving myself for Jesus. And yes, it's as fucked up and gross as that sounds.

When you make me come, I don't want to be reminded about how for so long I was saving myself for marriage. How I prayed, every night, that my future husband was saving himself as well. How I hoped he remained pure for me, but if he didn't, if he slipped up here and there, it was probably okay because he was a man and the main focus was *me* being intact, not him. Lord willing, I would be the first vagina my future husband would stick his dick into, but it would be fine if that wasn't the case. He'd be forgiven.

Don't freak out when I tell you I haven't had a lot of sexual experience. That definitely won't make me come. It'll make me get all neurotic and self-conscious, which is just my default state of mind anyway, seeing as how I'm a Puerto

Rican and Italian girl from Philadelphia. Let's call a spade a spade: I was born having a panic attack, so I don't need any added anxiety while I'm trying to enjoy an orgasm. It's not like I didn't *want* more sexual partners, it's just that when you spend every night journaling in your Christian diary about your future spouse, you miss out on a lot of opportunities to fuck.

Which brings me to the next point: I'm trying to *enjoy* it. You should know, going into this, that I associate sexual pleasure and coming with guilt and shame. They're all hand-in-hand thanks to the Christian church, which terrified me into staying a virgin for a long time. Because Jesus sees everything, right? He's always right there, over your shoulder, especially anytime your hand creeps below your own underwear because you want to explore yourself and figure out why your impatient boyfriend can't make you feel good.

So I'm *trying*. And if you want to make me come, know that I had to give myself a pep talk before being this intimate with you. I had to tell myself, over and over again, that it was okay to feel like a sexual being. That it wasn't something to be ashamed or embarrassed about, that God wouldn't smite me, which is something I spent most of my life being afraid of. Who, me? Just your average American woman, being constantly terrified about God smiting her to damnation.

Don't make me feel stupid for the fact that it hurts. I know, I know. Sex hurts when you first start having it, but know that I just want it to *happen* and I don't want to focus on the pain because it's looming over my head, making me feel broken as a woman. Because I want to be able to fuck my partner like anyone else out there, but I can't because my body literally rebels against me every single time I try to open it up to someone. It rebels because that's what I taught it to do for so long, afraid that if I gave in to the pleasure and the feeling then I was being a bad person. Sex was meant for a husband and wife, and it definitely wasn't meant for feeling good. So it's only natural that every time I feel good, I freak out and close up and it creates this barrier between us, over and over again.

Let me guide you. Let me show you how I want to feel. Christians try to make each other feel guilty about masturbating, but it's what saved me during the time I was a Bible-thumping, evangelical young woman. Don't be intimidated that I know my own body. That I know what drives me over the edge. Let me teach you.

Be patient. Please. I know you don't get it because you've never had to deal with this. You've never had to deal with feeling like something is physically wrong with you because you want to have sex and you want to have an orgasm but you *can't* because all you can focus on is your youth leader telling you how fucking screws you up. So please, be patient with me. Which, to be quite honest, should just be a damn given, but a lot of people don't seem to understand this. If you're patient, I will come... which sounds like a line from a warped version of *Field of Dreams*, but it holds the most truth, and I will probably say this all the time, loudly and confidently, so get used to it.

Know that I'm learning. I'm learning and changing and growing every day, little by little, peeling back the layers of shame that have been forced on me. I'm learning what my body likes…I'm learning that I won't be banished to hell for touching myself, for showing you what I want, for communicating these things. I won't go to hell for having an orgasm.

Also, just please don't talk about Jesus.

"Get in there. Get messy."

There are many different ways I can come. Sometimes I want us to make love and look longingly into each other's eyes. Most of the time, though, I want it rough and playful. Below is a checklist for you to refer to. Read carefully. xx

How to make me come: A checklist

- ☐ Music is optional.
- ☐ Alcohol is optional.
- ☐ Clothing is optional.
- ☐ Kiss me passionately. Don't be too precious about it.
- ☐ Let me believe I have the control sometimes. I want you to beg to fuck me.
- ☐ Spend a lot of time on foreplay. Grab my tits. Kiss down my stomach. Come back up. Tease me. I want to beg you to fuck me.
- ☐ Do not start fingering me aggressively right away. I'm not wet yet and it hurts. And not in a good way.
- ☐ If you want to finger-fuck me, please make sure your nails are cut and you have taken off all rings, if you wear any. (I'm not talking about wedding rings. If

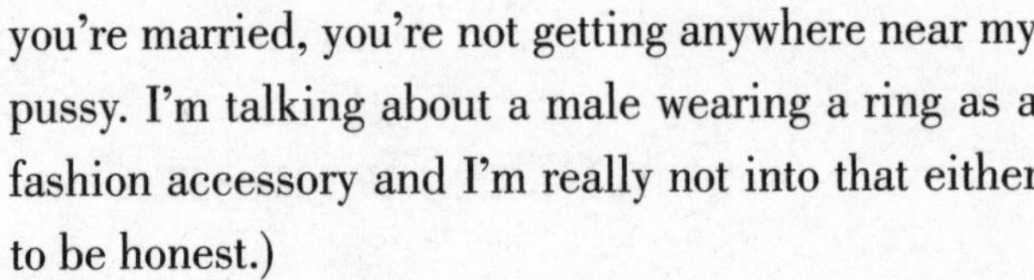

you're married, you're not getting anywhere near my pussy. I'm talking about a male wearing a ring as a fashion accessory and I'm really not into that either to be honest.)

- ☐ Tell me I'm incredibly sexy and you can't control yourself around me.
- ☐ Choke me until I am about to come and just when I'm about to, release your grip.
- ☐ Let me touch myself while you are:
  - ☐ a. Fingering me.
  - ☐ b. Fucking me.
  - ☐ c. Literally any time you are doing anything to me.
- ☐ If you are going down on me, please use your fingers, too. Massage my G-spot. (Don't worry—I'll guide you there and I'll be very vocal when you find it.)
- ☐ If you are going down on me, use your whole mouth. Get in there. Get messy. The whole area around my clit is incredibly sensitive and wants to be touched, too.
- ☐ Let me sit on your face. Keep your tongue out so I can rub my clit on it. Don't be passive while I'm riding your face. Grab my ass. Smack it. Grab my tits.
- ☐ Do not repeatedly ask me, "Did you come yet?" When I do, you will know.
- ☐ Continue to check in with me. Look me in the eyes. Read my body language. We are in this together. I want this to be fun. I promise if you make me come, I will return the favor wholeheartedly.
- ☐ When you first enter me, go slow. This is another

great time to tease me. Rub your dick against me. Let me feel my wetness on you. Put in the tip and slowly fill me with all of you.

- ☐ Don't think of sex as a sprint with coming as crossing the finish line. Let's take some of the pressure off. Let's explore getting there together.
- ☐ If I'm on top of you, put one hand right above my clit (where my pubic hair is/would be) and put your other hand on my ass. Now, if you push and pull me as I grind on you, you are exaggerating my movements, getting even deeper inside me.
- ☐ Tell me I'm yours and ask me to come for you.
- ☐ Put my legs over your shoulders and thrust deeply while I rub my clit. This is the perfect time to try combining a few things, i.e.: choking, looking me in the eyes, telling me how hot I am, asking me to come for you, etc.
- ☐ If you are fucking me from behind, smack me hard on my ass.
- ☐ If all else fails, just hand me my vibrator and tell me I'm pretty.

"Slowly, I began to realize that as guilty as I felt about sex, I also really enjoyed it."

I have a very conservative view about sex. About orgasms. About how many sexual partners is an acceptable number. About it all. It comes from always wanting to be the "good girl"—the one who does the "right thing." And it's not something I'm proud of. In every other facet of my life, I'm a very liberal human being. I long to approach sex with a coolness and a sort of unaffected whimsy. However, in the words of Lady Gaga, "I was born this way"—with the world and my actions weighing heavily on my fragile and emotional shoulders.

In elementary school I would hold self-imposed nightly "confession sessions" with my mom. I would tell her my sin of the day, and she would tell me what I needed to do in order to right each wrong. My sins varied from littering to lying, and my mom would listen and then tell me how to solve each problem. The following day I would do exactly what she had told me, and you know what? It worked. Repenting always made me feel better. But as I got older, and the problems got bigger, I found myself more and more alone. I mean, you can't bring your mother into bed with you. Or I guess you can, but that just isn't my style.

The first time I had sex I was seventeen. I went back and forth trying to decide if it was the right thing for me. I was in a committed relationship with a guy I loved, so why not? I was extremely nervous, but truly believed that I would feel different afterward. I thought I would be embraced into a new world of womanhood with a warm hug and open arms. And that's exactly what happened. Oh wait, none of that happened—just the sex part. The next day my boyfriend of two years broke up with me, providing even more proof that sex was bad and a mistake and not to be enjoyed.

It took me a few more years before I even wanted to try it again. This time I did it with a very loving and caring boyfriend, who, shocker, did NOT break up with me afterward. We just continued to love each other emotionally and physically. Slowly, I began to realize that as guilty as I felt about sex, I also really enjoyed it. And that's a hard thing (that's what she said) to reconcile. The truth was and is that I like having sex, and that's okay. In fact, it's more than okay, it's great! I like the feeling of intimacy that is created within the act. And I. Love. To. Come.

But this still isn't without complications. A guilty conscience follows me through each relationship, tryst, and one-night stand.* I am still trying to navigate through a minefield of right and wrong. Should you sleep with a guy on a first date if you think there's potential for a more serious relationship? How many partners is too many? Does it

---

* I've actually never had a one-night stand. The one time I tried, I ended up dating the guy for six months.

matter? It shouldn't, but somehow it still does to me. And should orgasming be the goal of sex, or should you just appreciate the act itself?

I continued to ask myself those questions as I sat down to write this, and then I did what any smart, thorough, type A writer would do—I did my research. And by that, I mean I masturbated. I got under the covers, holding my vibrator, as more thoughts and questions started to form. I thought about what felt good and what I really needed in order to get off. I began to realize that I honestly couldn't tell you what it is that really gets me going, or what it takes to finish me. Maybe just a good vibrator? There are just too many factors! My mood, how I feel about my body, did I shower that day, am I too full or too tired? All these thoughts begin to flood my mind. And that's on top of my already guilt-ridden feelings about sex.

The same is true when a guy tries to make me come. My brain is loaded with questions about him and me. What do I look like from his angle? Do I taste bad? Is he enjoying this? Is he getting tired? He must be tired. Is his tongue hurting? Should I just tell him to stop to put us both out of our misery? "You get an A for effort but honestly, it's not you, it really is me and my fucked-up brain." Should I just pretend I came so we can both be over this awkward moment?

Do guys worry about this when you're going down on them? I can say that based on my own experiences, they most certainly do not. I've never once had a guy stop me in the middle of a blowjob to tell me it just isn't going to happen. They just push my head up and down in order to make me go faster. So why do I put so much emphasis on how my partner is feeling?

All I can say is that I'm trying. I have come to terms, more so with my own sexuality. I can own the fact that I like sex and that when I do feel comfortable with a guy, I want to do it all the time. But I still can't reconcile that guilty conscience. It's somehow lingered and sometimes brings me back to being a little kid and feeling like I'm doing something wrong.

I am thankful to the kind men I've been with who have been sensitive and have listened to my body, even when I have a difficult time doing so. And I'm definitely thankful for my trusty vibrator, for it continues to support me unconditionally, which I hope I can one day say about someone that doesn't take AAA batteries.

"I'm sure I'm not the only one, but every single guy I hooked up with attempted to have anal sex with me."

I suppose I should probably begin by saying I started my sexual experiences at a pretty young age. It doesn't seem as important now that I'm older, because it really only means I've been doing this for a while, I learned how to enjoy sex pretty early on, and I'm not shy about it. I was the one my friends came to for advice and now I'm the one they know they can tell anything without judgment. I'm willing to try most things at least once or twice. I'm not big on relationships; I've had one serious boyfriend and a lot of random hookups, fuck buddies, friends with benefits, whatever you want to call them.

With all of this in mind, I'll tell you that a few years ago something strange started happening to me. I'm sure I'm not the only one, but every single guy I hooked up with attempted to have anal sex with me. I'm not sure if it just suddenly became a trend or if there's something about me that specifically says, "Hey, I'd love it if you shoved your giant dick up my ass." Let me also say that none of these guys asked, they just did; as if the act wasn't bad enough, it was always a surprise!

The first guy tried to act like it was an accident, like,

"Oh, sorry, wrong hole," but then proceeded to do it again, so he wasn't fooling anyone. The second guy ended up being gay, so that makes a lot of sense. The third guy came prematurely the first time, so why he even thought he might have needed a smaller, tighter place to stick his (smaller than I usually go for) dick I'm not sure. The last guy was this man I met on Tinder. Let's call him Thomas, because that is what my genius friend calls him.

Thomas was something else. We chatted for a while before we met, and he was very nice—a little too nice, if you ask me, so I was prepared for him to end up being a horrible asshole. We met one night when he suddenly decided he *had* to meet me. I promised myself I wasn't going to have sex with him that night because he was sooooooo good-looking and I was kind of into him. Yes, I know it was dumb since we met on Tinder and were both clearly just looking for a hookup, but let's just say this was a really stupid time in my life and leave it at that.

Anyway, we met, we hit it off immediately, we made out A LOT. We went from the bar to the street to a bench to my stoop, where I continued to fight the urge to drag him up to my apartment, rip off his clothes, and have my way with him. Naturally I thought the best thing to do was unzip his pants and give him head on the steps of my apartment, and let me just tell you his dick is one of the biggest, most perfect dicks I have ever seen in my life. Perfect length, girth, you name it. I'm kind of drooling a little just thinking about it.

Clearly, after getting down on my knees in the middle of

the street, I was finding it hard to remember why I wasn't going to have sex with him in the first place. The embarrassing and real reason was that my apartment was a disaster. I had just gotten home from vacation and there were clothes thrown everywhere. Needless to say, I gave in and we had incredible sex twice that night. He continued to text me the next day and the entire weekend after that while he was on vacation with his friends. It started with pictures of the view, videos of him and his friends playing beer pong, normal cute "I just met you and I'm into you" kind of stuff. Until the next morning, I was at the restaurant where I work, setting up, when Thomas texted me "good morning." I couldn't believe it, this guy and I met once, had sex, and it was great, sure, I thought we would probably hook up again, but this was boyfriend behavior. I responded with something really cute, no doubt, and then he said something about wishing I was there, followed by NOT a picture, but a DICK VIDEO! I kid you not, first he outlined it with his hand inside his navy-blue boxer briefs, then he pulled it out and stroked it a little. I screamed, mostly out of shock—sure, guys had whipped their dicks out in front of me on the street, talked dirty, tried to have anal sex without asking—but NEVER had I received a dick video. Everyone at work was very curious; none of them had ever received one either, so I showed it to them. To be fair, Thomas knew I was at work in a restaurant with a staff of people; did he really think I wouldn't show them? I honestly think he wouldn't care if he knew now, he is clearly very proud of himself. I guess I would be, too.

After that weekend we talked on and off but didn't see each other again until about a month later. We met for drinks, and in the Uber back to his place, I somehow ended up giving him head again. There was just something about this guy that made me want to do things I wouldn't usually do. I was so much less inhibited with him. And then it happened: he pulled my head up and whispered in my ear, "I wanna put it in your ass tonight." ARE YOU FUCKING KIDDING ME?! I'm sure that was the first thought in my mind: not this literal shit again! But I just giggled and blushed and said, "I think you're too big for that," because honestly, that was a real concern. He laughed and said, "No way," and kind of dropped it.

Cut to us having sex on his bed. Hallelujah, it was worth the wait! After we finished we smoked some green, got insanely high, and started to do it again, only this time, he went for the ass. I let him do it, since, to be honest, everything felt so good with him I figured I'd try again. I coached him, reminding him to go slowly, but as soon as he got more into it, it was way too much. I must have whimpered or let out some sort of hurt-animal sound because he stopped and asked me if I was okay. He was holding me and I was shaking, probably the most vulnerable I've been around any man who wasn't my one boyfriend. He was sweet and kept apologizing. We had sex again the next morning and it was great. To be honest, I get confused about what happened which time we hooked up, but I remember at the time thinking how it was the best sex ever.

What I remember now is that every time we hooked up,

he stuck it in my ass, and every time I stopped him after a couple of minutes. One night I encouraged it, because I was so turned on and probably on some extra drug or something so I thought I might actually like it. It still hurt, I bled, got shit all over myself, and ended up getting a UTI. I also remember that he never made sure I was wet, he always just grabbed me by the vagina and started fucking me, which ended up leaving me very sore and with a burning sensation for a few days afterward.

I also realized he never, EVER went down on me. Now, I'm one of those rare women who actually prefers intercourse to being eaten out. I love the feeling of having something inside of me pounding away, but that doesn't mean I don't also enjoy a little foreplay. Foreplay makes everything feel better. Whether she gets off from intercourse or not, it never hurts to eat a girl out a little. I wasn't really mad about it, but when I think about all the times I went down on him in public, in private, once for the longest I've ever sucked anything in my life (I'm not sure how long it was but it felt like at least half an hour)... after all that, he couldn't go down on me once? Or even throw a little spit on there before he just rammed his penis into me? We hooked up a handful of times, and every session we had sex three times. That's at least fifteen chances... And nothing.

We stopped seeing each other because he started dating someone. He still reaches out to me sometimes. I don't answer. I hope his girlfriend enjoys being fucked in the ass. I honestly don't know what I would do if I saw him again. I'd probably fuck him. But this time, I would tell him how to do it right. Honestly, the best thing that came out of the whole situation was that he made me realize just how much of my self-worth I had lost.

I knew he liked having sex with me. I would get on top of him and ride him because it felt so good, and because I could see his shit-eating grin and how much he loved it. One night while I was on top of him doing some of my best work, he told me, "You fuck like a call girl." I don't know exactly what he meant. I don't know if he really knew how a call girl fucks, but I enjoy sex when it's good. In the moment, I took the comment as a compliment, we were both enjoying ourselves and it was kind of hot, but the longer I thought about his "call girl" remark, the more it irked me. Sure, I like a little dirty talk, I love a little rough play, but why is it that when women "have sex like a man" we are disrespected and looked down upon, treated like sluts and prostitutes? When a man does it he is celebrated, revered, a baller, a pimp.

First of all, I hate the phrase "have sex like a man," because if I wanted to have sex like a man I would buy a strap-on and go fuck someone. What I do, or at least what I want to do, is have sex with a man whom I respect, somewhat enjoy as a person, but don't necessarily want to be my boyfriend. I really don't want a boyfriend right now. I come from a family of divorce—in fact they are still in the process—and it is nuts. I am in my mid-to-late twenties and living the real struggle of being an artist and supporting myself with a day job. I don't really have the time or energy to delve into emotions and feelings with someone right now.

Honestly, I love too hard for that. But I am a smart, educated, openly sexual woman. I know this isn't a new topic, I've read many an article about it, but for some reason, it isn't totally clicking.

I hear men saying, "I wish I could find a cool girl to hook up with on the regular, just keep it casual." I am that "cool girl" and I can tell you that is not what they really want. What it seems they want is a sex robot who will do whatever they want with no concern for herself. Of course, not all men are like that. I recently hooked up with a guy from another country and he was insanely respectful, so conscious of taking care of me, every girl's dream, right? The bottom line, I've come to realize, is we are in charge of ourselves. You are an adult woman doing adult things; no one is going to take care of you. If you don't like something, speak up! Don't be shy or worried about making things awkward, because a guy who is worth any time at all will respect that and try to understand, and a guy who doesn't is probably a selfish asshole anyway so good riddance. If men want to see the open, sexy, I'll-try-anything type of women they fantasize about, they need to learn to respect and please these women as well.

"Dogs and cats gotta be off the bed."

Dear Past, Present, and Future Men with Whom I Have Been or Will Be Intimate,

Hello! What a strange feeling to be talking to you all at once, but here we are. I hope you're all doing well and I hope whichever woman (or man) you're currently being intimate with is also doing well and is well satisfied.

First things first, I have a confession to make: I haven't been completely honest with, say... 70 percent of you. You were led to believe that you made me orgasm and I'm so sorry to say... you did not... ahem... cross the finish line. For whatever reason, I decided that I wanted you to think that you had gotten me there. I'm so sorry for tricking you. And what's even worse is that all of you believed me! I'd like to think that that was due to my phenomenal acting skills, but let's be honest, that's probably not the case. Without getting too deep into it, what's more likely is that you were never properly taught how to give a *real* orgasm. We, as women, have been taught that our sexual needs and desires should come second to yours. What this leads to is a hesitancy to demand what we want (and deserve) in the bedroom. So I am here to teach you how to give one! Well, give one (or more) to me, at least. To the 30 percent of you who have gotten me there... THANK YOU. But it probably wouldn't hurt for you to have a refresher course, either.

Before we get physical, let's address how I need to feel emotionally before anything happens. I need to feel safe. I need to feel like you won't judge and will even be into the faces and noises I make. I need to feel like you won't care if I didn't have time to shave that day. I need to feel like my needs aren't something you're just getting out of the way quickly so that we can move on to yours.

I need to feel wanted. I want you to be super into whatever is happening and super into me. I need to feel like you want nothing more than to run your tongue over every inch of me. If I'm letting ANY part of you go inside of me, it means that I *want* you. It means that I want to be the one who makes you moan, I want to be the one you go inside of, and I, ultimately, want to be the one who makes you come.

A few more quick tips before the nitty gritty: I can be buzzed, but not super drunk. If we're in a bed, it helps if there is more than one pillow. Dogs and cats gotta be off the bed. That one sounds obvious, but I've actually had to say, "Look, they've gotta go. This won't work if he's lying between us." Let's follow each other's lead when it comes to the dirty talk. I like confidence. It tends to kill the mood a bit if you're constantly asking, "Is this okay?" All socks have gotta be off.

I like having my neck kissed. I like having my neck bitten. I like having my ear kissed. I like having my ear bitten.

If I tell you to do anything harder…I REALLY mean it. Whether that's biting, slapping, or thrusting. Let me be the one to tell you if it gets too rough.

In the words of the great Amy Poehler, "If you don't eat pussy, keep walking." Only one man has ever made me come purely through penis-in-vagina penetration, and that was after three years of sexual tension between us. I'm not doing that again. Ninety-nine percent of the time, I can't finish if there's no oral involved. If you're eating me out and I tell you to kiss me, do it. I like the taste. Let your fingers take over. But I won't protest if you resist at first. The idea that you couldn't possibly tear your mouth away from my clit is, let's be honest, really hot. It speaks to the whole "being wanted" thing.

And finally, I like to know what makes you feel good! I want to make you come just as badly as I want to come. It's a two-way street. Let's walk it together, buddy.

So I hope this has been informative for all of you. Feels great to get this all down on internet paper. Before I hit the sack with any future lovers, it's going to be SO much easier to just link them here rather than talk about my feelings. Plus, it will make a lot more sense when I push their heads toward my vagina and scream, "Amy Poehler said to do this!"

xoxo
—me

P.S. If worse comes to worst, and you are just truly not up to the task: Hand me my vibrator and turn on some Justin Timberlake. I'll manage just fine on my own.

"An ex and I timed it to see how long it would take for him to make me climax: seventeen seconds."

Orgasms and I have a complicated relationship. I'd relate my orgasming skills to those of a fourteen-year-old boy. If I'm turned on—and not drunk, mind you, because in that circumstance the whole system pretty much shuts down—it turns into a battle between me and my vagina not to come. Over the years it's gotten better. With practice I've been able to last up to fifteen minutes into sex without coming. Of course, that usually involves a lot of pausing while I make loud, unsexy hissing noises signaling to my partner not to move a muscle (well, a very specific muscle).

It all started about twenty years ago, when I was six or seven years old. I was lying on my stomach on my bedroom floor, listening to my sister's boom box, when my stomach started to itch. Being both lazy and creative (two words that would come to define me for most of my life), I pulled myself up and down using the carpet to scratch my stomach. It definitely scratched my stomach. *Definitely*. Do I need to put a little winky face to really clarify what I'm trying to say? I orgasmed. I thought I was dying. I asked my mom if there was something wrong with me because I'd "felt something funny in my stomach." I really don't know if she remembers that conversation, and for both our sakes, I pretend I don't. That conversation is unfortunately one of my strongest childhood memories. Surprising, really, since the embarrassment of it wouldn't sink in for years and years.

She never explained what had happened, she just laughed and told me I was fine. I didn't have any urge to experience that feeling again. Not until the Herbal Essences commercials came out and I proceeded to hump everything in the house. After that, I wasn't very sexually active (with other people, I mean) throughout high school. Then I discovered people *wanted* to have sex with me, and again I proceeded to hump everything.

And here is when I discovered my inability to last longer than a couple of minutes. You see, you need context. Up until that point, for all I knew, that was what sex was like for everyone. And it is, if you're a thirteen-year-old boy discovering a JCPenney catalog for the first time, but not for most adults with some sort of control over their bodies. An ex and I timed it to see how long it would take for him to make me climax: seventeen seconds. I come quickly during sex, I come when I'm making out, and if there's enough movement and enough tightness in my jeans, I'll come while we're hugging.

If we've made out, there's a 50 percent chance that I came. I wouldn't have said anything. Your only clue would've been my abrupt and unexplained sudden disinterest. *'Cause that's the thing*. Being intimate and close with someone during sex is beautiful and romantic and blah blah

blah, but once that momentum is gone, so's my—and let's be honest, *most people's*—interest. Don't get me wrong, I love getting guys off as much as the next gal, but love of the game only gets one so far. Once they take the points off the scoreboard, players are going to start walking off the field. I'm not sure I really *get* sports metaphors, but I think my implication is clear: it gets boring.

But all this excessive backstory actually has a point. I think my quick orgasming has directed my sexual taste in a very specific way. Maybe I'm wrong. Maybe I would be just as into the things I am if it took me three hours to come, but I doubt it. Over the years I've developed a variety of depraved and perverted things that turn me on, but the first fantasy that really took off and stayed with me, the one that's still with me today no matter how much I indulge it, is being teased. I don't mean light touching or leading up to and then postponing the inevitable. I mean I want to be right on the edge of coming and have it snatched away from me. I mean I want all that amazing buildup with none of the payoff. To put it plainly, I want to be used.

I want a guy to fuck me until he comes, never once taking into consideration my needs, and then just leave me there unsatisfied. I love being held down, tied up, used. Not even free enough to please myself. I like having to beg, being forced to do whatever comes to my partner's mind just to get him to let me come. Honestly, just reading my words, I cringe at how crass they are, but I've had so many years of the following evenings: we make out, I get turned on, we start to fool around, I orgasm, and then I flatline for the next fifteen minutes to an hour. I mean, I'm probably in better shape because of it, but an hour? You try orgasming and then still having to hump something and/or someone for another sixty minutes; you cramp up.

What I want is to earn my orgasm. I want it to take time. I want to come so close that it surprises me when it slips away.

Sex for me is all about the buildup. It's my absolute favorite part and almost every time it's the thing I miss out on. Orgasming is great, being close is great, but my sweet spot's in that space in between. Whether it's because I'm tied up and turned into some little sex kitten or there are those flattering hissing pauses every fifteen to thirty seconds, it's what I'm looking for. I want to live in that period where your hands can't reach enough places, where your lips can't get close enough, where you're so turned on you could run a fucking 25K marathon (is that a thing?). That's the place where it all comes together.

SOFTER

"Love me like Sting loves Trudie."

To make me come you're going to have to be a woman, bring a woman, or know how to use your body and mind like a woman. So ladies, you're in luck! It shouldn't be hard to get me there, and you don't need to be hard to do it. Gentlemen, there's still hope. Mechanically my body will still respond to you, and I may even enjoy our sex (a lot!), but you'll have to work a little harder than your feminine counterparts. Basically what it boils down to is that with women, my sex is usually mutual, meaning I can easily participate in pleasure while I give it. With men, I prefer to be worshipped, pleasured and pleased and treated like the goddess I am. My general rule is that your "ticket for admission is one orgasm." Don't expect to put it in me until you've worked for it!

And so, ladies and gentlemen, this is how to make me come.

When we get to the bedroom, let's make sure we're alone (unless we're having a threesome, in which case, fuck yeah) and are able to communicate with both moans and words without your roommate playing N64 in the living room. This level of intimacy isn't always easy-breezy for me, and while sometimes it's hot to pretend we're fifteen-year-old girls at sleepaway camp trying not to get caught, in general we'll have more success if we choose a location that fosters intimate trust. I don't drink alcohol any longer and one of the reasons is because my sex SUCKED when I drank, and often I would fake orgasms to get it over with. I was disconnected from my body and anxious to get off to make my partner feel accomplished. Girls, and guys, didn't matter. I was scared of my own pleasure. Eventually I started to assume I just couldn't come very easily, or that something was wrong with me. Over time, I've reconnected with myself, my needs, my wants, and it turns out I'm entirely capable of coming—but us both being sober helps a ton! Being on the same page is very adult, and very cool.

My main request, no matter what you've got between your legs, is: LET'S TAKE IT SLOW. Tempo is everything. If you wanna make it great, you'll wait. I'm into the idea of building up our sexual energy slowly, walking that divine tantric line. Love me like Sting loves Trudie. Kiss me for ten minutes before you decide to brush your hand over my nipple. Let your tongue in my mouth remind me of what you're going to do to my pussy. Watch my body language, 'cause I'll start to beg for your touch. If you aren't sure that I'm begging, let's talk about it. There's nothing hotter than telling you what I want, and you listening. I'm the type that needs some intellectual stimulation—best-case scenario, you're whispering in my ear what you want to do to me. If that's uncomfortable for you, literally just telling me you want me or asking me what feels good is a fantastic start. I'll let you know what I want.

So we've been making out for a while, and that's great!

Even once I'm writhing against you, continue to take your time. Experiment with qualities of touching and try to relax and know that we're creating this arousal together. This isn't me putting you to some test, this is one grand foray into the art of play and pleasure. You can try touching me lightly, slowly, in circles, in lines. You can try kissing me, licking me, sucking on my body, everywhere but my vagina. Save the main event for last. A word on my nipples: It's rare, but I've come just by being touched here, so WOW, please don't forget about them! Tug on them, bite them (gently!), swirl your tongue around them, embrace them, knead them, and then move on to the next one, and then back again. This will get me hotter than pretty much anything else.

When it's clear that I'm ready, you can start to use your fingers to venture downward. Explore my pussy, but please don't go straight for my clit. I'm not ready quite yet. The lips like to be rubbed, pulled, massaged. My actual vagina will probably be dripping, and dipping a finger in there is nice, but only to lubricate your exploration—don't penetrate me yet. Put your mouth down there and literally just breathe onto my clit. It feels great, I promise! Whether you want to start with your fingers or your tongue, I'll eventually say to you, "Eat me! Please!" in which case you'll gladly oblige and probably use both body parts. This game of teasing and playing makes me feel so wanted, so loved, and like my pleasure is so important to you. It doesn't really matter if we've hooked up twice or for two years, taking this time makes all the difference. Breathe with me. I know it sounds cheesy, but we're connecting on a pretty intense level, and again, being on the same page is cool.

At this point, if you've been using your hands, go ahead and use your mouth. Remember, tempo is everything—try a swirling circular motion, try going up and down or back and forth, try a tap, try a rub, try a tongue that flicks and then one that flattens. Whatever you do, remember that my clitoris is the most sensitive part of my body and so while it needs a nice touch, it doesn't need a firm one. You might be at this for a little bit, but that's all part of the fun. If you're a girl, we can sit on each other's faces and that'll probably take care of itself. If you're a dude, keep at it! I'm getting closer. Explore me with your mouth, like I'm the best treat you've ever had. When you want to be down there, when you're loving it, I can feel it, and it drives me wild. I just want to be wanted!

At this point, go ahead and slip one or two fingers inside me—but be gentle! Finger-fuck me in and slightly up, so that you hit my cervix. Steady and easy does it. I'd prefer slow to fast. Once we're here, we're in the homestretch. Stay steady, my gods and goddesses, and don't forget to reach up and fondle my breasts, showing them the love they deserve. Once you do, it will likely put me over the edge. Let me explode into your mouth, and then put your mouth on my mouth, and kiss me until I'm either dying to return the favor or ready to open up to be fucked 2.0. If we're going there, we're going to have to do some more touching, some more loving, some more patient connecting, but I can come with you inside me with the same amount of attentive love-making. Do all of this and then repeat. Forever and ever, amen.

"YOIRM—Your Orgasm Is Ruining Mine"

As a woman who has been having orgasms since she was probably six or seven years old, it may seem a bit weird that I have a decent-sized list of all that comes in the way of that. Isn't it funny? When you think of all the things that women have to go through physically, emotionally, culturally. And then there is the most natural of pleasures—even that has to be complicated. But nevertheless, she persisted.

I didn't grow up in a liberal household. My mother never talked to me about sex. Quite the opposite. She wouldn't let me watch anything that was remotely sexual. Covered my eyes or told me to cover them myself. You know how badly I wanted to watch *Dirty Dancing*? She wouldn't even let me watch the opening credits because you see somewhat of a silhouette of two people dancing super close. I don't know what age I was when I finally watched it. But it was later than everyone else, dammit! Anyhoo, this went on until I was a teenager. So, in that way, I am lucky. I say that because while my mom was keeping me away from one of the greatest movies ever, I was still climaxing on a pretty regular basis.

I took pornography in any form I could get it, and from pretty early on, too. I think I was eleven or twelve when I started reading one of my mom's mystery books, *The Third Deadly Sin* by Lawrence Sanders. There was an erotic scene with the main guy and I must have read it at least ten times in one sitting. It was my go-to for a while. As I got older, mystery novels would turn into pornos, which would later turn into a temporary subscription to the Playboy Channel, which is funny being that I am a straight woman. But any which way to enjoy myself was a pleasure that I was unabashed by.

I couldn't tell you why or how I was so comfortable with my sexuality. I certainly was insecure about my appearance, which you would think would be an issue. And you know that I didn't grow up in this sex-positive home (cue *Dirty Dancing* soundtrack). I wasn't one of the cool kids, or one of the cool adults for that matter. But taking claim and having a stake in feeling turned on and doing something about it always was my own. I never saw anything wrong with it. And I indulged in it often.

I got older, and fooling around with boys turned into having sex with men, which you would think was a big difference. Surprisingly, it wasn't. I'm not here to bash men. Certainly not. I don't envy them one bit. Giving a woman an orgasm is ridiculously challenging. And the men who think they're so great at it, the men who think they have this one unique move down...sigh. How they've been lied to! For a while I thought women were ruining my sex life. All these women would fake orgasms to either spare the guy hurt feelings or to have a painfully boring session come to a close or just to get home in time for *Game of Thrones*.

Either way, these women, my sisters in the human race, would lie to these men, making them think that what they were doing worked, giving them a false sense of ego and pride, possibly making them a wee bit narcissistic. And then do you know what happens? Those same men, with those same falsehoods, come into my bed, do something absolutely bananas, and are clueless as to why it isn't working. "You're the only one this hasn't worked on." No, kind sir, I am not. "No, really, you are." Nope, I'm not. I promise you, I am not. There was a period of my life where I heard versions of this so often that as I lay there after, unsatisfied, I daydreamed about going on tour to cities all over the world asking women to stop faking it. I was going to call it YOIRM—Your Orgasm Is Ruining Mine. I tried for different acronyms but that was the best I came up with. Aside from sounding like a boy's name in Hebrew, it's not terribly catchy.

However, there is more to the story than YOIRM. I never orgasmed with *any* man I fooled around or slept with. And this was a problem when I knew my husband was going to be my husband. How was I to go the rest of my life sleeping with a man who didn't bring me to climax? I was in therapy at the time and I talked about this with my therapist. He asked me if I was able to have an orgasm on my own, and I assured him I could. So, once it was confirmed that all parts worked down there, he was pretty sure that my lack of climaxing was due to a lack of trust. "I trust him," I responded, completely aghast at what he was suggesting. "You trust him to be loyal, to be honest. But you don't trust him where you can be completely vulnerable." Hmph. He was right. He was always right. Who thought about orgasms and vulnerability in the same sentence? To me, an orgasm was just a wonderful response to some very methodical friction. But it does make you vulnerable. And I guess I didn't trust that I could be that open with my boyfriend and that he still would be interested. Strange but true. So, I go to his place after work, same day as that therapy session, and I let myself be vulnerable. And wowza. Wowza, wowza, wowza. We both were so happy when I came that I think we were ready to marry right then and there. No joke, I am pretty sure I saw doves fly from behind his head. Beautiful white doves.

I'm lucky. I'm lucky because I know a lot of women who have never orgasmed. Who don't know how to ask their partner for what they want, who don't feel comfortable masturbating. For one reason or another, they have a lot of shame. And, unfortunately, there are a lot of ways for that to happen. So, here they are, women well into their thirties and their norm for a sex life is orgasmless. It's expected to not have an expectation. It's something they can live with because that's how they've lived. It's a damn tragedy. I don't mind saying so.

Listen, it doesn't matter what country you live in, what era you were born in, what kind of relationship you may be in—when you're alone, be it in your room late at night or on the couch when your roommate leaves the apartment, you are free. No one is watching. No one is judging. Your body, every bit of it, belongs to you. And that pleasure, no matter how elusive, is yours. All yours. It's there for you to enjoy every fragile, wonderful second of it. Even if it's coming from your mom's favorite mystery novel.

> "She explained to me that I had one of the few known strains of HPV that can lead to cervical cancer."

"What do I do now?" I said, lying flat on my back. It was my first time having sex without a condom and I didn't know the protocol. A few months prior, my boyfriend had suggested that I start taking the pill in hopes of worry-free sex. I was resistant to the idea, but it seemed to make sense logistically; we were two healthy and horny twentysomethings in a committed relationship. I joined the leagues of dedicated women who take the pill daily. I set an alarm on my phone and cracked open the foil packet to reveal a small but life-altering decision.

There was no part of my twenty-three-year-old self that wanted to take the pill. Over the two years prior, I had realized that I live in a highly sensitive and responsive body. I became vegan, I traded shampoo for baking soda, and I skipped the painkillers when I got my wisdom teeth pulled. While some would call these lifestyle choices strict (if not militant), I felt a sense of freedom from my previous choices, which had given me anxiety and too many hang-overs. Nothing entered my body that wasn't pure, non-GMO, and organic—except the very low dosage of hormones that I took every day. I felt a tinge of shame when I would admit to others that this was part of my sexual regimen, but beneath the superficial bruise to my ego was a deeper misalignment with my beliefs and desires. I knew I didn't want to take the pill, I just couldn't pinpoint *why*. As the months passed, I enjoyed the perks of our new sex life. My boobs went up a cup size, my skin cleared up, and I enjoyed the closeness of our bodies without the thin layer of latex between us. I had successfully quieted the small but distinct voice of resistance in my mind. Plus, my boyfriend was happy. Despite all this, I still felt an internal uneasiness. Being on the pill started to feel like more than just a lie, it felt like a betrayal.

Several years and one breakup later, I sat in the gynecologist's office receiving the results from a routine Pap smear. I had been diagnosed with high-grade cervical dysplasia as a result of HPV. Up to that point, HPV felt like something that had affected everyone in my sphere but me. I had heard my girlfriends' tales of abnormal Pap smears, but they didn't seem too concerned, casually whispering over coffee in between other bits of gossip ("But like, everyone has HPV"). It always felt more like an episode of *Girls* than a serious health issue. In most of their cases, the abnormal cells had returned to their normal state over time without intervention. With my friends and in the media, the general consensus seemed to be that HPV wasn't a big deal.

It wasn't until I sat down with my doctor that the gravity of the situation body-slammed me. She explained to me that I had one of the few known strains of HPV that can lead to cervical cancer. She held her arms apart to demonstrate her point. “On a scale of zero to cancer you’re here,” she said, putting her fist right in the middle. It seemed like in the ocean of no-big-deal strains of HPV, I had a big-deal one. My first reaction was fear; my second was anger. I wanted to blame someone for infecting my perfect body. I automatically started questioning the integrity of each man I had slept with. Part of me felt victimized, that this was unfair because of my low number of sexual partners. I was responsible! I was healthy! I had listened to those annoying ads and gotten the HPV vaccination years before (at the time, it didn’t cover the strain I had). I also felt frustrated that my partners couldn’t be tested for this, and that another woman would potentially suffer. All roads of inquiry led me back to me and choices. I was fucked, and not in the good way.

Aside from surgery, conventional medicine didn’t have many treatment options. A common method of removing abnormal cells is the loop electrosurgical excision procedure (LEEP), during which the cells are cauterized with an electrical wire. Thinking about this procedure made my stomach clench up like a fist. I had long since thrown away my last packet of birth control pills. My sensitive body was almost back to feeling balanced in its natural state. I didn’t want to disrupt that progress. I imagined how traumatizing this procedure would be for me. Something told me I could heal this another way. I decided to give myself time to seek alternative treatments. My doctor reluctantly gave me the thumbs-up to explore other options, but warned me that if the cells hadn’t improved by my next checkup, I should seriously consider removing them. I felt a distinct transfer of the reins into my hands; my health was my responsibility and no one else's.

One of the many steps toward healing came as part of a European vacation. I traveled to a well-known center that offers holistic treatments. Their approach was simple: bring the body back into a state of balance and it will heal itself. I dove headfirst into treatments, all day, every day. I had a cow's fresh thymus cells injected into my neck. I liked to entertain my German doctor by yelling "*Mist!*" ("Cow shit!") each time he performed an injection that really hurt. I figured out which modalities resonated with me (muscle testing: fascinating) and which didn't (colon hydrotherapy: humiliating). I cried. A lot. I learned that the HPV vaccination had been banned in certain countries (Japan and France, among others). When I would return to my small hotel room at the end of the day, I'd cram in phone calls to my family and binge on Netflix until the Wi-Fi shut down at seven. At a certain point, I think I'd actually forgotten that I even had a vagina, never mind that it could be pleasured. It was more like something I noticed at the bathhouse, suddenly self-conscious in the presence of naked seventy-year-old European men. My vagina had become something clinical, a tunnel that doctors peered down to determine how close to cervical cancer I was. While I felt healthier, I knew I had only scratched the surface. I wanted to go deeper than the virus and the abnormal cells, to get to the root of what had caused this rebellion in my body. I started to wonder whether masturbating in my hotel room every night for two weeks would have been a more productive (and less expensive) treatment. But I didn't want to make love to anyone, least of all myself.

When I returned to the United States, months went by and I continued on my regimen from Europe. Herbs, supplements, IV therapy, vaginal suppositories, acupuncture, yoga, the works. I found a naturopath to work with in addition to my Western doctor. Physically, I felt great. I had full faith that what I was doing was working, even if I couldn't see the results. I opened up about my process to anyone who wanted to know. I realized there was so much confusion surrounding HPV and cervical dysplasia. It was like this invisible network that affected everyone yet connected no one. Women seemed frustrated by their lack of options, and nearly everyone I spoke to seemed to have conflicting information gleaned from friends, the internet, and their doctors.

Then there was the issue of sex. I discovered that many women, like myself, felt that HPV had caused them to feel fear, mistrust, or general apathy around sex. Sex was no longer desirable but rather a physical act that had caused them to suffer. I had begun to think of sex as nothing more than an object repeatedly bumping up against my cervix, which, at the end of the day, just wanted to be alone. I knew that my relationship to sex was a key part in decoding the mystery of how to heal, yet I had barely started to unearth the psycho-emotional aspects of my condition. I had always been introspective, but this was a whole other level. I felt that the great internalization of my emotions mirrored my sex organ, invisible from the outside, complex and buried within. There was no clear direction to turn. I took a breath and began to dive deep through the layers, swimming into the core of myself.

After almost a year of treating myself without surgery, I had another biopsy done. I sat on my balcony as I received the call from my doctor, tense with anticipation and excitement. This was the moment I had been waiting for. I had dedicated a year's worth of energy to this issue and I was confident that all my effort would pay off. I would finally be able to relax knowing that I had carved my own way, with everything on my own terms. I broke down the moment I heard the doctor's voice. The cells hadn't advanced, but they hadn't regressed, either. They were at the same stage. I lay down on the floor of my balcony, unable to move. My doctor strongly urged me to have the LEEP. She explained that I was on the border of pre-cancer, and that there was no reason to let the cells progress if we could prevent it. I knew she was right, and yet I still felt a resistance in my body. I had tried nearly every healing modality with dedication and conviction, but maybe there was something else I could do. While I was happy that I had stabilized the condition, it wasn't enough to be optimistic. I scheduled the removal of the cells for the following month.

The month before the procedure I felt completely defeated. Each day that passed, I sank deeper into a sadness that blurred my world gray. The only time I felt remotely normal was when I went into my meditation practice for long stretches of time. Yet during this time, I also felt a sense of relaxation knowing that there was nothing else to do but wait. A voice arose from within that said, *Surrender*.

A week or so later, I sat deep in meditation and a warm pool of energy collected at the base of my spine, just below my sacrum. I breathed into this energy, and it started to arouse me. I instinctively started moving, gently circulating the energy upward, though not physically stimulating myself. What followed was an intense sensation that came in waves; it rose up my spine and penetrated my chest. I felt my heart expand open as wide as the universe. It was an orgasm devoid of sexual context, an orgasm of pure love. In the months following this experience, there were days when I felt as if I was vibrating for no apparent reason. I was deeply turned on by everything. Anything could inspire arousal—watching the beauty of a flower falling from a tree or sinking my fingers into grains of sand on the beach. Even just breathing deeply seemed to induce a heightened state. It was like having foreplay with myself. Making love became an experience of any moment, not just a sexual act. I realized I didn't need a partner, or even stimulation. What had caused me pain and suffering was actually the modality that healed me. Sex was my medicine and I was my own lover.

After this experience, I knew something had changed physically inside my body. I still had the LEEP procedure on the calendar, but I had the urge to postpone it. I couldn't bring myself to ask my doctor, knowing she would probably think I was crazy. How could I explain that I had healed myself in my own living room? My last checkup had only been a month prior and it was very unlikely that the cells had improved during that time, considering that they had stayed in the same margin for a year. Still, I could feel that something had shifted deeply. I told myself if I were to go forward with the procedure, I had to be one hundred percent behind it. I didn't want to think of it as a concession, but rather an empowering choice for my ultimate health. I needed to let go of my ideals and step forward with fearlessness. It was time to integrate past and present, truth and betrayal, masculine and feminine, the parts of myself I adored and the parts that hid in shadows. I was all of it.

The LEEP procedure was painless and easy. I sat in my car after for a few moments after, passive tears crawling down my cheeks. I felt an energetic door close behind me; I knew this chapter had come to an end. A few days later, my doctor called me with the pathology results. I sat on my balcony once again, but this time, breathing deeper than ever before. Her voice was unnerving, a combination of confusion and astonishment: "The cells have regressed, actually," she said. She went on to explain what a pleasant surprise these results were and to keep doing whatever I was doing. An inner smile of gratitude spread throughout my body. I knew I couldn't explain my process and that I didn't have to. I thanked her and hung up. I sat there for a long time, resting in the sound of an empty space.

"Kiss my nipples and tell me they taste sweet."

How to make me come

Hands-on time: About 15 minutes
Recipe makes: 1 or 2 orgasms

Ingredients

- You
- Me
- A soft bed

Directions

1. Preheat. Want me. Tell me you do. This will make me want you more. Be literally unable to keep your hands and mouth off of me.
2. Shower me with compliments. *Genuine* compliments. Go beyond "beautiful" and "sexy." Tell me my breasts are peachy orbs of lusciousness. Tell me my eyes are like the sea. Kiss my nipples and tell

me they taste sweet. Tell me you can't stop kissing them. (Note: I get bored after too much breast play, but I like knowing that you can't get enough of them.)

3. Lay me down. I don't want to be standing or even sitting for this. I want to be on my back. If there are too many pillows on the bed, throw them on the floor. Pay attention to my comfort. This is important, and you will be rewarded.
4. Kiss my mouth and neck (pay a lot of attention to the neck) while you gently stroke the slightly rounded space between my belly button and pubic bone. For whatever reason, I have a huge concentration of nerve endings here, and playing with it will simultaneously relax me and turn me on.
5. Pull my underwear off and throw it on the floor.
6. Reach down and gently comb your fingers through my pubic hair. It should be exciting to you that I have it—if you prefer a smooth labia, that's cool but please get the fuck off of me.
7. Begin gently stroking my clitoris, toward the top.
8. Keeping one finger on the top, move a second finger to the top left side. Keep stroking.
9. Don't be discouraged when I ask you to be more gentle. My clit gets overwhelmed very easily, and I'll need you to decrease pressure when that happens. You can slowly rebuild the pressure as I get more and more excited, and then decrease again when it gets to be too much.

10. Keep going. I'm blessed with a highly orgasmic clit, so three to four minutes of stroking, building up and then backing off on the pressure, should get me there. I'll probably start playing with your cock as I get more and more turned on, but as I near orgasm, I'll be unable to multitask and will stop to focus on my pleasure. Don't worry, I'll return to it shortly.
11. As I get ready to come, it's important that you don't change anything. If you move your hand or shift the direction of your stroking, I might lose the feeling. Please stay as you are. I'll likely whisper, "Just like that. Just like that."
12. Keep stroking through the orgasm, through my bucking hips.
13. As soon as I've come, I'll push your hand away. I'll be too overwhelmed and won't be able to handle any action for about thirty seconds.
14. Once I've recalibrated, I'll want to have penetrative vaginal sex. I'll climb on top of you, or you can climb on top of me. We'll feel it out in the moment.
15. Because I've just come, I'll likely have a shorter but still very intense orgasm from penetration after just a few minutes.
16. At this point, my focus turns to making you come.

"I was so inhibited that I did not talk about sex with him or even birth control."

How I have felt about orgasms with a partner since my adolescence...

Age sixty-four, in a monogamous relationship (a marriage) for thirty-one years.

Hormones and interest in boys. Coming from a strict Catholic background, there was tremendous conflict about wanting a boy, experiencing my hormones as a thirteen-to-eighteen-year-old and staying in the virgin zone. Heavy petting was what I considered wild. I wanted to be desired and enjoyed being flirtatious and feeling attractive. I was more interested in how I was coming off to my guy, liking to feel erotic and teasing him rather than focusing on mutual pleasure to orgasm. Intercourse was out of the question. I was wearing a chastity belt mentally although my behavior may have been arousing and I was surely aroused.

The college years for me were the early seventies. My interest in men was more about the mystique of having a full-blown sexual relationship. I fantasized about it and felt totally insecure about it. I had a continued fear of getting pregnant and also a fear of being "used" in losing my virginity unless I was at least engaged to be married. I felt a lot of pressure to have sex with my long-term boyfriend, whom I met a few months before my nineteenth birthday. I was repressed; I felt inadequate sexually with this handsome, virile partner who, I realize now, also felt inadequate sexually. We were not interested in communicating sexually or giving each other pleasure. It was more like we were trying out our sexual selves to work through our inadequacies. It felt good physically to be making out and engaging in coitus interruptus (and playing Russian roulette with pregnancy and a pregnancy scare). I was so inhibited that I did not talk about sex with him or even birth control. By the time we did have intercourse when I was twenty-three years old, our relationship had withered beyond repair. The lack of a growing and blossoming sexual relationship intertwined with other issues made that so. I had expectations of marriage; he wanted a hot sexual experience with a different kind of woman than who I was.

We broke up a few weeks before our wedding date (luckily). I felt scarred emotionally and felt totally sexually inadequate and rejected. I was hyper-focused on my inability to deliver sexually. It took me years to recover and grow from that experience. Therapy helped me work out some of those feelings. Enough to feel I could trust a man to really want me, for me to allow myself to relax enough with him to think of my pleasure. I have had to learn to take responsibility for my sexuality and my pleasure.

To think of my pleasure and relax and enjoy . . . all

important ingredients to achieving orgasm. I have had orgasms with my husband and some short periods of sexual satisfaction. My marriage has gone through many low periods—poor communication, my husband's clinical depression, my own depression, the difficulties of child-rearing . . . The good news is we have worked through hurdles on all these fronts. I do feel loved. I feel healthy and energetic enough for sex. I want to be enjoying it into old age. Currently, there is warmth and affection but no sex. My man's own inhibitions, performance anxiety (?) and struggles with feeling controlled by me have been and to some extent continue to be barriers to that pleasure zone. I can only work on me. I go through periods of feeling sexual and then not. Now it is really important for me to keep in touch with my body, my sensuality/sexuality, and my own affirmation of my physical self because I still want a sex life that is more than fantasy and self-stimulation. I do let my man know I still want a vibrant sex life and that I love him. The rest of the story is still to be told.

"I've only been having sex for about five years, so I still have a lot to learn."

Dear future lover,

First, a few admissions:

1. I have faked orgasms on several occasions.
2. I have had (and hope to have more) sex with both men and women.
3. I lost my virginity when I was twenty-one years old.

I start with this to say that I fully accept my part in any sexual miscommunications I've experienced in the past; that I don't yet know my sexual preferences within my sexual preferences; and lastly, that I've only been having sex for about five years, so I still have a lot to learn. I hope you find this useful because I would very much like to start having really, really awesome sex with you.

Let's start here: I'm new at this.

I don't have sex often, so my vagina is tight. Good for you. Painful for me. Take it slow! I once had a roommate with a deviated uterus and she had more sex than I'm currently having, just to give you an idea. Be gentle. Times when I've faked orgasms are when my vagina is being brutally pummeled and I am so overwhelmed that I just fake-shake my leg and break up my moans into really short bursts just to get it all over with. I've also faked orgasms in less extreme situations, but it always comes down to my clit becoming desensitized by an uncommunicative partner. Why didn't you speak up, you ask? I know, I know. Communication is great, but I'm new at this, remember?

Speaking of which, new equals exploration. So let's explore. Don't just plop yourself on the map like we're at an IHOP. Maybe *my* hot chocolate doesn't come with whipped cream, jah feel? I've had sex with guys who assume that just because I have a big butt (I get it from my mama) I like anal or would love to ride dick. On a real tip, though, I have weak ligaments in my knee and an irritated back from an old pulled muscle, so we're gonna have to find a better position than that!

One last thing on this "brave new world" note is that I've found and keep finding that I am sexually attracted to more than one sex. So far, I've had sex with men and women but I've gotten wet-panty syndrome from a few transgender folks as well. I am still exploring my sexuality, and as a result, sometimes I'm feeling penis, sometimes I'm feeling vagina, and this can very much affect whether or not I am going to actually enjoy having sex with you. How is this in your control, you might be asking. I don't know quite yet. Maybe you can ask me what I'd like for dinner that night and we can go from there? SUSHI!

Moving right along: I've experienced both the good and bad of being a little kinky.

The best sex I've ever had was in a bathroom at a party at a house in Koreatown. No shade. It was hot! How about me and you get a little dirty, huh? It was the first time I had successfully done a vertical vaginal doggy style and my God was it amazing. This worked so well because the guy and I drunkenly communicated our desire for immediate satisfaction and the sex was passionate and animalistic. It felt rebellious and exhilarating, but yes, with the good kink comes the not-so-good.

A couple of months ago, a friend of mine convinced me that trying polyamory with him was a good idea. In my naïveté, I thought that if I didn't at least try it (that is, have sex with him as *he* practiced polyamory) I would be a prude and never find my sexual niche. It was an awful decision. When he told me to sit on his face, all I could think was *What the hell am I doing?* Then I sat on his face. The thing that jolted me out of enjoying it was not that I was having sex with a friend or that I had somehow convinced myself that I wanted to be with someone who was with several other someones, but that he was talking dirty to me in the most inauthentic, general way. Sit on my face? I...just...can't. Again, this could totally be PG in the world of getting it on, but to me and my sexual lustrum, it felt like a subjectified stereotype of a sexual experience. More interested in playing out an idea of what it should feel and sound like, we missed the present moment of being intimate. Bad on him. Bad on me. There is a real opportunity for sexual experimentation, but this taught me that without an enormous amount of heart, these experiments can fall flat and be extremely unfulfilling. I want to experiment with you, so help me to bring passion and authenticity into it.

Last thing I want to tell you: my pillow has been the only thing that has consistently made me come.

Characteristics that my pillow possesses that keep me coming back for more: it's safe, reliable, and firm. I guess we can end on a few things I've learned from Hank... I mean, my pillow. One, I need to know that I'm safe and that my sexual experience or lack thereof isn't going to lead to some immediate judgment of the intimacy that we can have in a present moment. Two, I need to know that you can be reliable, ya know? That once I go down on you or let you rub your clit on my butt until you come, you won't roll over and put your underwear back on. I am trusting you to care about my needs and work with me to get them met. And three, I need you to be a firm lover. Merriam-Webster defines *firm* as "set, placed, or attached in a way that is not easily moved; not weak or uncertain."

Dear lover, take note! Be firm with your love, with your emotions, and most of all with your physical embrace. I want to trust that you have *me* and that you see *me* and that you feel *me* and not just your boner or the last time you had sex or that thing you are doing later. Make an effort to stay present with me throughout our sexual intimacy and I promise that I will try to do the same. I am a bisexual woman who lost her virginity at twenty-one and who often fakes orgasms except when dry-humping her pillow. I hope this helps you make me come.

Love,
Me

"I thought that it was an urban legend that couples come together, but we both come very quickly."

I feel very lucky—from what it seems from talking to my friends, I come relatively easily for a woman. I am a cis heterosexual woman with a steady boyfriend and we usually have sex every day. I almost always need clitoral stimulation, but don't necessarily need a lot of time for it. I can come from missionary and girl-on-top without stimulation like a hand or a vibrator, and can come from doggy style if I'm masturbating at the same time. I would say that I could probably come every time I have sex if I take long enough. I don't really need visual stimulation—I like to close my eyes sometimes to remove distractions. When I'm not in a steady relationship I masturbate all the time, and can come two or three times a day. I don't use sex toys at all, which is mostly due to laziness but also because just using my hand seems to work. My favorite orgasms happen during sex. I like it so much more than either oral or fingering. I've never had anal sex and don't have any real desire to. My boyfriend and I often come at the same time, which is insane. I thought that it was an urban legend that couples come together, but we both come very quickly.

I used to have the horrible habit of lying about coming,

though. I would never turn down sex with a boyfriend just because I was tired or didn't feel like it—I thought it was my obligation to at least pretend to enjoy sex all the time. In retrospect I feel like this is slightly duplicitous or at the very least not helping myself get what I need. Because I come so easily normally, I think it was easier to fake an orgasm, since it made sense. I think partners (in my case, straight men) need to realize that it's not a race to orgasm, and also that sex can be "good" or "successful" without both partners coming. Sex can take an hour and that's great. I have started being so much more communicative as I get older because it makes sex better for everyone. As clichéd as this sounds, when you are pleasuring your partner you feel good. My boyfriend and I go down on each other almost every time we have sex, and it makes it so much better for both of us. Women should be bossy about what they want—not only will it lead to better sex for them, but my partners at the very least have seemed to find it sexy.

"There's a very fine line between kissing breasts in a super-sexy way and making it feel like a man is feeling super oedipal and trying to breastfeed."

Attraction

He must be confident and energetically engaged. He needs to make me feel like I am his only object of desire and that there are no other distractions. If he looks at his phone or other women, I start to slowly check out of whatever momentum we have. Desperation and timidity are turn-offs. Giving me 100 percent of his attention is the biggest turn-on. I love it when a man is direct about what he likes about me physically and mentally. Even though I'm not planning on having children in the immediate future, I feel the biological and primal undertone of nature's course: I am generally attracted to men with large and clear eyes, full lips, strong jawlines—all the subliminal signs of being genetically strong. It's extremely attractive for me when a man is healthy and cares for his body.

Foreplay

Foreplay starts with any direct sexual conversation and any type of touching. My neck (specifically the back of my neck) is an incredible nerve hot spot for me, so I like it when a man holds me from behind and kisses me there, also reaching around to touch my breasts or finger me. I love deep openmouthed kissing when we are standing, as if we are slow-dancing with our bodies pressed firmly against each other. I like for the man to accent the hourglass shape of my body as he touches me by holding the slim part of my waist. There's a residual fantasy I have left over from being a Catholic school student, which is that the "reaching up the skirt" motion is a huge turn-on for me. Generally, undressing should be part of the sexual act and it's often wonderful to see how far we can go before the clothes are completely removed.

Oral pleasure

A great blowjob position is to have me lying on the bed and him standing behind me. He has a full view of my body and I am giving him an upside down blowjob.

I also enjoy giving a blowjob to a man when he is lying in bed and I am by his side kneeling in a straddled position so that he can see my whole body that way and has access to touch my breasts and finger me. This position offers a similar dynamic to 69-ing, where there is a mutual interplay of rising tension.

Being held from behind during foreplay can be fantastic because he can touch my breasts with one hand, finger me with the other hand, and kiss the back of my neck. When I give a blowjob, I like to focus on the feeling of friction on my lips and experience a giant turn-on from that.

It's difficult for me to come from oral pleasure unless I am also giving my partner reciprocal pleasure at the same time. 69-ing is one of my favorite things, but I prefer to do it in the dark where our other senses are heightened more than vision. There's something about the act of receiving that can make me feel too queenly or worshipped... I prefer to be pleasuring him at the same time.

Breasts

There's a very fine line between kissing breasts in a super-sexy way and making it feel like a man is feeling super oedipal and trying to breastfeed. Kissing the nipple and all around the breast up to the collarbone is a great move without actually suckling the nipple. Moving wet fingers in a circular motion around the nipple is also one of my favorite feelings in the world.

The clitoris: The key to orgasm

I prefer some clitoral stimulation at the same time as penetration. Depending on the man's penis size and body shape, it's often possible to stimulate my clit by having his penis deep enough inside me that our pubic bones are grinding against each other if I am on top or we are in missionary. If it's from behind or any side variations, I usually touch my clit or allow him to do that at the same time. In nearly every sexual encounter I've had, the man and I orgasm at the same time. I think that because I've developed a very solid communication with my body through yoga, meditation, and exercise, I have a good amount of control over and awareness of the timing of orgasms. I like him to say my name when he comes, which is also part of that "only object of desire" idea.

I'm interested in sexual reflexology, which involves sending the sexual energy into different areas of the body. I've never had a partner as interested in this as me, so it's usually something I've just played with on my own. There's something called a microcosmic orbit meditation that allows partners to heal each other and move energy through each other's bodies.

Intensity/intuition

Be intuitive with your woman. If you're interested in getting rougher, try a little bit at a time and be receptive to her responses. It's okay to ask permission to try certain things, to be open, to laugh together when there is a funny or awkward moment. Just be confident and engaged and give her your full attention. Become one with her. Be honest in your physical actions and intentions. Make her feel safe and she'll bloom for you. Be her safety net and she'll allow herself to rise for a transcendent experience.

Unexplored fantasy

A few of my unexplored fantasies involve having sex in a sensory deprivation chamber, or just a room that is so totally pitch black that our senses other than vision are extremely heightened. I'd love to have sex on a dock near a body of water. I'd love to have sex in the back of a car parked at a mountainous view. There are so many things I'd like to try.

"I forget about how much I like sex, so if you want to make me come, remind me."

Have you ever put a cup of coffee in the microwave, completely forgotten about it, and then found it again, hours later, patiently waiting for you?

That's how I think about sex.

I love coffee. I need coffee. I love sex. I need sex. But sex is rarely front of mind for me—I am much more concerned and consumed by what I should wear to the wedding we're invited to next weekend or if you've made your optometrist appointment yet or if we will ever be successful enough to move out of this tiny apartment or . . . or . . . or . . .

You think about sex much more than I do. You are an objectively hornier human being. This is (one of many reasons) why I love you. Why I need you.

Sex makes you feel loved and connected and relaxed. I don't feel deserving of love or connection or relaxation before I've finished my mental to-do list, which is endless. I know it's backward. I'm working on it.

I forget about how much I like sex, so if you want to make me come, remind me.

Pry my phone out of my hand. Lie down with me and let's talk about our days until our breaths are full and even. Then let's fuck the way we like to, the way we always do, we know what we're doing by now.

Days from now if you feel like I'm "not interested," trust me, I am still in the microwave. I just need you to heat me up.

"I don't want to be having sex where faking an orgasm is the only way out of it. I don't want to be having sex where I even NEED a way out of it."

"Let me know when you're about to come and I'll choke you."

Those were the words that led to my first, and only, full-on fake orgasm. In short: It was a one-night stand and we'd had a very lighthearted, playful (or so I thought) conversation earlier in the night about *Fifty Shades of Grey*. Fast-forward to several hours later and we were in a hostel bunk bed having mediocre sex and he was telling me I was about to get choked. I don't know if this was elicited by our previous conversation or if this was his go-to line, but regardless…it did not turn me on. At all.

I lay there for a few minutes trying to figure out how I wanted to play this. I never really felt nervous about the choking (although in hindsight, I absolutely should have…what were you THINKING, twenty-four-year-old self?). It was more that I really just had no desire to be choked by a stranger, on top of the fact that I knew I was never going to have an orgasm at any point during the experience. I wasn't very turned on to begin with, but more significantly I have never had an orgasm from "regular" sex. I have had many, many orgasms in my life.

From masturbating, from oral sex, from fingering, from dry-humping. But vaginal penetrative sex is never the way that I can climax. Good sex can feel earth-shattering, jaw-droppingly good, but I still won't get an orgasm from it. And so the fact that this guy just assumed that a) I would definitely be having an orgasm, and b) choking me would help AID in said orgasm, made me just want it to be over.

My conclusion was that if I could achieve the end goal faster, the whole thing would end faster. And so, very suddenly, with no warning whatsoever, and while holding his hands tightly above my head as far from my neck as possible, I faked an orgasm. There was nothing about it that made me proud. It didn't feel victorious, and it certainly was not meant to boost his ego. Rather, it was just a means to get out of doing something I didn't want to keep doing.

I haven't had many conversations with other girls about faking orgasms. Maybe that's because it really isn't something to be proud of, or maybe because when it does happen it's likely due to a subpar sexual experience that's not worth writing home about. But I do know this: I don't want to be having sex where faking an orgasm is the only way out of it. I don't want to be having sex where I even NEED a way out of it. I want guys to know that having an orgasm is not always simple or easy. I don't want them to assume that it's going to happen for all women and during each and every sexual encounter, and in some cases, it may not happen ever. I want them to understand that if a woman seems like she is really enjoying sex, she probably is! But that still doesn't mean she's definitely going to climax. And in that vein, if we don't climax, don't be offended—just ask questions to find out what will help next time. Ask us, "What turns you on? What feels good? What do you want me to do?"

Don't be afraid to have a dialogue before, during, and after sex. Ask us questions, and when we answer those questions, LISTEN. Any woman is going to appreciate a man who is attentive to her sexual needs and wants. Anyone can fake an orgasm. But really hot, highly pleasurable sex where both people are on the same page because they've checked in with each other and are honest about what turns them on—that's about as real as it gets.

"We have all been made to feel powerless or weak in sexual circumstances. Let's commit to not perpetuating that."

I am a twenty-seven-year-old, white, cisgender, femme, queer (but often passing as or assumed to be straight), able-bodied, formerly fat, bighearted, California-grown human-ass being. And I am a survivor of many forms of sexual assault. That's a truth that I've been working with more and more and I'm proud as shit to say I am healing all the parts of me that were hurt, shamed, and hiding, and I am now loving *all* the parts of me. And I've been doing whatever else I felt I needed to do to move forward and not have those wounds define me.

One effect of all this is I'm no longer interested in casual sex. It turns out that "casual sex" was almost never actually about my pleasure. And I only realize now how dangerous and impossible it would be for me; for my safety and well-being. So you, who may be my lover, you should know that I am not a casual lay. I am not a no-strings-attached, easy, whatever you may wish, Pussy to stick your prick in. Nope!

And as I write this, I need to make it known that I am not only turned on by people who are grown-ass Men, but I am also turned on—incredibly so—by women and those who do not identify as just one of these two genders.

Having said that, I do feel that women and other people who hold a good amount of feminine wisdom do not need the same kind of information I am presenting here. So though I personally embody a sensual, sexual, feminine spirit that LOVES, adores, and grows relationships with people of all gender expressions, this very serious and very lighthearted talking-to is directed at dear ones who identify as Men.

So, as I was saying—I need to, like, *get to know you* for some stretch of time before we get to dick-in-my-holes fun. You know, so it might actually be fun for both of us. That's the reality that I'm operating within. One in which we are adults, so we get to choose!

If you want to get close to me, that's great and beautiful and yes, I actually am really interested in getting to know wonderful people, intimately even, but it may be a long while before we get super intimate physically. Or it may not be so long, I don't know! There will probably be long conversations, though, before any sex acts. We'll have to talk and listen and be honest and vulnerable with each other, please. Otherwise no pussy magic fun for you.

Along the way there will probably be sweet make-out sessions, delightful building-of-companionship sensations, and maybe massages, tickle attacks, and/or hand-holding! So that's exciting. (It is pretty exciting for me...)

So can I explode the myth that you need to "make me" come? Yeah, nope. Sorry, I don't get down with that phrase. For me, "coming" is not anything that sounds like another person controlling my body or taking the reins and deciding

When and How. It's a co-creative process! I'd like to release some of that pressure, for both our sakes.

I can "make" myself come anytime I want. But being with a partner is not just about getting to the "coming." The orgasm moment is not the Goal. Got that? I reiterate: One Orgasm does not equal One Finish Line. Did your brain explode a little?

Climaxes (multiple!), physical release, and bliss will indeed happen, if we allow ourselves to go there together. And personally, I need to feel comfortable to play with my partner and luxuriate in the eternal moments that swirl around those climaxes. There will have to be power dynamics, shifts, and one of us leading and one of us following, and switching it up and doing what feels right. Sometimes that may feel like compromise because this is a true collaboration, and it may even feel like you (my partner) are giving up some of your power and control to me. At this time in the story of the world, I say that's probably a good thing to do more often. We can both let go, and also consciously allow me to voice my choice more of the time. Join me in smashing the patriarchy. Even within our bedroom endeavors.

Most women have been hurt and abused in some way in intimate spaces, so try to bring that into your awareness before entering into sexual intimacy with me, or with any other person. *We have all been made to feel powerless or weak in sexual circumstances.* Let's commit to not perpetuating that.

Even if I want you to take the lead or "fuck me hard" or "do whatever you want to me," or anything else one of us speaks aloud that is reminiscent of letting the other person dominate—we can always make sure we act upon a clear request, with my (or your) choice and verbal consent. We make tons of choices together in the acts of lovemaking and in those long conversations before (which is pretty cool foreplay if you ask me). We choose to verbalize these things not just out of necessity, but also because *it is a turn-on* to speak your desires and ask for something explicitly.

I personally cannot get down with intense surprises in the sack. For example, I don't want you to start calling me "bitch" out of the blue while we're having sex, when we haven't discussed that as being a turn-on. That did happen (paired with some really unwanted physical aggression) and it majorly sucked. That's just not okay.

Again, we're adult humans. Try on a little empathy for me. If we haven't shared stories specifically of my past and what I've survived, please do not assume anything about me or what I carry with me in my memories and in my body.

You know what is hot? It is so hot when you communicate well and listen with compassion.

It is really very hot when a guy knows what he likes and isn't afraid to talk about it in an open, honest, vulnerable, and clear way. When he's facing whatever resistance, insecurity, fear, or baggage and still courageously dives into the act of opening his heart and his truth to me...oof, that gets me tingling right there in the space between my clit and vaginal opening.

It also really turns me on when it feels like there isn't a ton of excess baggage, subtext, unreasonable expectations, bending of the truth, or game-playing going on between us. Holy fuck, that'd be brilliant.

Well, actually, maybe certain kinds of game-playing would be nice... but only when we both know we're playing the game and that it's intentional and ultimately meant for pleasure.

I would like to feel met. Like, meet me, right here where we are. Not just "meet me halfway" or "Hi, nice to meet you," but, sure, those things, too. I'm talking more about soul recognition, partnership, and just a simple willingness to dive into something side by side as unique individuals but equals. Like a friend you can hold hands with as you jump off a crazy high cliff into a mysterious body of water.

It turns me on when I can feel that you see me. You hear me. You accept me. And you are at least trying to "get" me. You're also trying to be met by me, be seen and heard in return.

Please, meet me in our amazement of each other. Meet me in our fear too. It's only natural to have some fear. Maybe we're dumbfounded at times. That's cool, too.

We may even come up a little short. We may discover that we're not compatible in some way, and decide to not be lovers anymore. That might be painful, awkward, challenging, all of that. This is life. But at least we are not lying to ourselves, or to each other.

And at least we're both alive and trying. And, ultimately, we are on the same team.

I seek a partner—a teammate—in passion and pleasure.

I want to create a safe space together, so we can both lose our minds and *feel more in our bodies*.

A lot of what I'm getting at boils down to this plea: *Help me to feel not so alone.*

That's what my body yearns for. The times I can remember feeling the need to fake it or lie to my partner and say I reached climax when I didn't quite, that was when I had felt separate and alone, and in judgment of myself. Those times when I felt I couldn't be fully honest, I couldn't experience that rush and release of pleasure because I didn't feel safe and met.

Intimacy can be a gorgeous, ecstatic, embodied, restorative, blissful, unifying encounter. Let's try for more of that together, and stop perpetuating old patterns of wounding, shaming, and alienation. It's okay with me if it's awkward at times. It probably *has* to be, to get to the sweet stuff.

So let's build an honesty bubble together, okay? Bedsheets below and above us, protecting and billowing, as the sails on this Relation Ship we create and navigate.

Maybe that's cheesy as fuck, but it's real for me. Now tell me what's real for you.

> "Sex in my early sixties came with the agreement that it just didn't matter if either one of us had an orgasm."

How to make me come—if you insist

Oh sure; orgasms can feel sooo good. I remember the good ole days of simultaneous orgasms with the men of my youth. I remember those as the best. After that came the days of taking turns: he makes me come and then he gets to come. That worked; especially if we had intercourse; then I could come again. Sex in my early sixties came with the agreement that it just didn't matter if either one of us had an orgasm, "We weren't making babies, after all." (I know, it makes no sense.) So we would have sex for quite a long time, stopping for rest periods and going back for more. It felt really good. Sensations would get stronger, *ohmygod ohmygod ohmygod I'm almost there almost almost*... I could be in that almost state for a really long time. I might come or the arousal might just... wane. Sometimes we just kept at it until we were too worn out to continue. But it was a shared intimate experience, fun and oddly satisfying.

Does aging mean that the excitement of new-relationship sex wears off more quickly, or am I just faster to lose my illusions of romance after all these years? It did start to get a bit boring and I found myself considering having sex as a sleep aid. Then there's sex as brain exercise. When, in my mid-fifties, I looked into the eyes of my adored and adoring second husband and told him that I really didn't think I was going to come that time, he answered that I "must concentrate, darling." Ah, I thought: I have to *concentrate* to come! Otherwise I am disappointing him. And I really didn't want to do that. So I devised strategies to divert myself from the sense that it was a task: sexual fantasies, often with what would seem afterward to be humiliating scenarios. It is my opinion that feeling acutely embarrassed in a fantasy during sex sends the blood to important extremities; the clitoral equivalent of red ears, which leads to engorgement and kaboom.

The business of having sex now that I'm in my late sixties entails a lot of acceptance that a) I'm often just not turned on enough by my current partner to initiate sex, and b) this partner's erection is not that hard, or doesn't stay hard, or is just not going to come, so sex is going to be mostly manual.

Five years ago, after having been on my own for a while, I loved my personal orgasms with my mechanical sex toy. No serious concentration required. No worrying about whether he is getting tired or bored with trying to get me to come. And blissfully, no additional activity required after my vociferous release; just relaxation and sleep. Now, even using my really cool vibrator can seem like a chore; the orgasms seem perfunctory, coming too quickly and over too fast.

I like to think I could perk up some with new-relationship sex, especially if it could entail an honest-to-

God erection with a truly interesting and lovable man. Hard to say: I haven't met him yet. However rusty my equipment might be, I hate to think it's all over. I hope the excitement of being next to the right man might be rejuvenating. Here is how it might happen:

First, he takes me out to dinner and is charming and interesting. He is also genuinely interested in me. Not too adoring; this guy is comfortable in his own skin. When we continue the conversation at home, he might rub my feet and run his fingers up and down my legs or some other intimate gesture that will make us both want to go to the bedroom. When we're in bed, we both continue the gentle, quiet approach with lingering kisses and erotic touching.

Actually, I find our mutual arousal is the thing that really turns me on. Light stimulation, increasing in frequency and varying with placement, is the ticket for me; but most of all we are tuned in to each other. I want to find the thing that turns him on, too. When we are both aroused and ready, he probably has to enter me slowly so I can open up without discomfort—it's been a while. If he can stay hard as we continue, fantastic! I may need him to pull out and use his fingers to get me to come, but afterward if he can regain that erection and come inside me, fantastic. But actually, not completely necessary: if he wants me to finish him with my mouth, it would be my pleasure. If he doesn't come, so what? To be able to give each other this immense pleasure—with or without an orgasm—is a grand thing, and not to be taken for granted.

"I remember the day everything changed for me. The day I finally understood what tantra was."

"Men are like toasters. They heat up right away. Women are like ovens. They need lots of time," Bill says.

Bill is a seventy-three-year-old tantra master from New York, New York. He was sexually abused by a priest when he was a young boy, which led to a lifetime of alcoholism, eventual sobriety, and then tantra.

"Don't ever try to please your partner. Only do what feels good for *you*," says Marie, Bill's wife of ten years. "And whatever you do, *never* fake it. You can't catch the wave if you're too busy faking it."

Marie is a sixty-nine-year-old tantra master from Pasadena, California. She is a mother of three, grandmother of two, recovered alcoholic, and former prostitute.

A friend introduced me to Bill and Marie in 2013. I was twenty-nine years old and had hit rock bottom—I was having sex for money, while being in a relationship with an emotionally unavailable man who had no idea. I had been depressed and self-destructive all my life, suicidal, angry at my parents, jumping from one unavailable man to the next. I started seeing Bill and Marie regularly and they taught me how to love, forgive, and empower myself. They helped me face the reality of my addiction to men and sex. They supported me through painful withdrawal as I went without romance and sex for a year and a half. Meeting Bill and Marie saved my life.

And here I was now, with my boyfriend, Aaron, being guided by Bill and Marie. Aaron and I dated on a healthy dating plan, which meant we got to know each other, slowly, for three and a half months before ever having sex. Aaron was looking for the same thing I was—like Bill, he had been sexually abused as a child, which led to self-destructive and addictive behavior. He was the perfect partner for me. No judgment, no shame. He understood me, and I understood him. He needed tantra just as much as I did.

Tantra is the art of conscious loving. Tantra is the freedom from ignorance.

I remember the day everything changed for me. The day I finally understood what tantra was. What it felt like.

Aaron asked me if I would touch him. Down there. I said yes. Before this, I wouldn't have wanted to. Before this, I wouldn't have wanted to and would have said yes anyway. Before this, I didn't have a no. Before this, I thought sex was all I was good for.

But this time was different. This time, I was in my power; this time, I was ready. I thought of everything Bill and Marie taught me: I am a goddess. I do only what feels good for me. Out of my head and into my heart.

I had never felt anything like this before.

Seven years before this, I was giving a handjob to a guy in the back of his car for $200. Now, this wasn't a handjob.

This was lovemaking. I was doing it because I wanted to. Because it made *me* feel good. I went slowly, sensually. I was completely present. No chatter in my head. I felt a power I'd never felt before.

And then he came. And then I came, too. Before tantra, I never came. Before tantra, I faked it. Before tantra, I felt numb.

How do I come?

By loving myself. Choosing myself. Being responsible for myself. Empowering myself. By taking my time. Healing my shit. Facing my fears. Walking through fires. By forgiving. Accepting. Being honest. Trusting. Saying no. Knowing my partner. Liking, respecting, and trusting my partner. By doing only what feels good to *me*.

Every morning I wake up, I declare out loud:

I am a Goddess.
I deserve to have all of my needs met.
I deserve to have all of my desires fulfilled.

DEEPER

"He gets me off by telling me all about his naughty past with other women."

He finishes and he slides down my body, plopping down on the bed. I curl up next to him and get into position: right hand between my legs, left arm draped over his chest. I have my face turned up toward him and he, in the breathy aftermath of his own orgasm, begins to talk. "So, I'm in a park."

As he spins a sexy nighttime story, I begin to touch myself. The tales differ slightly in location, but the characters always remain the same. And I'm not one of them.

"I prefer a true story," I told him when we started to do this on the regular. "Tell me about a sexual encounter from your past."

"Really?" he asked. "You like that?"

"I do," I responded.

"You want to hear about me and some other woman?"

"Yes," I answered. "That's what I want."

I've been masturbating for as long as I can remember. During my childhood, it was completely nonsexual and simply something I did most nights before I fell asleep. I had a formula to my "feeling good," which involved lying on my stomach, wrapping my blanket around my hand, and bringing the bundle between my legs. I'd rock back and forth with my blanket-wrapped hand between my legs until a warm, cozy feeling erupted from my gut and spread over my entire body. I'd continue to lie there on my stomach, enjoying the fuzzies; after a moment, I'd roll over, extract my hand, and fall into a deep sleep.

Today, my masturbating method is almost exactly the same as it was when I was five or six. I lie down on my stomach with my hand between my legs (the blanket has long since retired, but once in a while a crumpled bedsheet proves to be an excellent, familiar partner in crime), and move my pelvis back and forth across my palm. There is, however, one crucial addition to the formula: I envision a sexy couple as I work myself. The woman has a killer body with gorgeous breasts and the man usually has a salt-and-pepper hairstyle with a firm stomach. Sometimes it's their relationship to each other that turns me on. He's the dean of student affairs, she's a top graduate student, and they have sex in his office. She's a senator, he's a journalist interviewing her, and they get it on in a beautiful hotel room. They're two ex-lovers reunited in Milan on a business trip. Or I recall in glorious detail the first love scene between Ralph Fiennes and Julianne Moore in *The End of the Affair*. My mother owned the movie on VHS and I'd watch the juicy parts in reserved, amazed silence some afternoons before she got home from work. This is all to say that during my masturbation sessions, I rarely imagine myself as a participant. Rather, I much prefer to watch two other humans do it on a desk, in a car, against the wall. Not in a porn, but in my mind with my eyes squeezed shut. Porn's okay, don't get me wrong; I do enjoy it once in a while. But truthfully, all I need is my own brain. I love masturbating. It's quick, it feels amazing, I know just what I like, and I always, always come. And come hard.

When I'm in bed with a man, the process is similar: I masturbate and he provides the images for me. I've only been brave enough to try this with my past two partners, both of whom have been a little confused but game. Prior to sleeping with these two men, my sexual encounters were chock-full of faking it—and one can blame that on my incessant need to tie up every situation with a pretty little bow. Ending sex with a whispery "Yeah, hold on, you can stop. I'm just not going to come" seemed pathetic. "Wow, yes, yes, that's it, oh my God, oh my God, yes!" conveyed something like *This was great, I'm so glad we did this, and I'd be down to do it again!* The guys were none the wiser and I felt content with the faking until I realized that, actually, maybe, it might not be so weird to ask a guy to simply tell me a story. It couldn't be that different from asking him to talk dirty to me (whatever that means—in my experience, asking a guy to talk dirty is just releasing his usage of the C-word thirty times in one twenty-minute sex session). After inquiring, "Really? You like that?" my current boyfriend has told me about the woman he fucked in a bar bathroom, another he met on an Amtrak, some threesome he had, plus a fictional fantasy about a particularly hot coworker. I've climaxed powerfully at every single drawn-out account. Sometimes he plays with my breasts, which feels great and helps me get there. Other times he tries to join me down below and I have to find a sneaky, sexy way to move his hand so I can continue the work on my own. I certainly love his fingers inside me when we start to fool around, but when it comes to having an orgasm, I need to do it myself.

To be clear: I've never had an orgasm during sex. Not even during oral sex, to which friends have exclaimed, "Seriously?" I've tried anal sex, which felt awesome, but still no dice. I've read plenty of women's magazine articles that suggest touching myself to understand how I come, but I totally understand how I come and it has to be by my own hand. It's a little disappointing; I wish my partner were more integral to the process. But he gets me off by telling me all about his naughty past with other women. And you know what, it's just what I enjoy. He *is* integral, in his own way.

"What do you like about that?" he asked me once. "It's the most...I don't know..." He trails off. "It's the most specific way to come. Why do you want to hear about other women? Why not yourself?"

I can't answer. Is it because I don't like to watch my own body? Is it because I don't like to be in my own body? If I thought myself more attractive, would I orgasm without needing to imagine people with tighter abs, tinier waists, and higher tits? Is this another way that I don't "live in the moment"? Do I have to literally extract myself from the current moment in order to come? Or is this my body physicalizing my need to do everything myself? Why can't I come when he's the one touching me? If I love this man and love having sex with this man, shouldn't I be able to let go in front of him? Shouldn't I be able to release myself over to him?

"It's just what I like," I say, and drape my arm over his chest. "Now, tell me the one about the girl from that cafe."

"I would take off my pants and undies, lie naked from the waist down on a table, insert a transparent plastic speculum into my vagina, and show a roomful of women I had never met how to do pelvic self-examination using a mirror."

The first time I heard the word *orgasm* spoken out loud was at least as exciting as the first time I had one. It was 1971 or '72, the height of the second wave of American feminism. Twenty or so of us were gathered in a community room on the Yale campus, attending the first meeting of an educational series on "Women's Health." The speaker, a nurse, stood at a blackboard, diagramming the female reproductive tract in anatomic detail. I'm pretty sure that night was also the first time I heard the word *clitoris* spoken aloud, with equally electrifying impact. Hearing these unspeakable words pronounced in public, at night, in a small gathering of women, was thrilling, impossible, a radical entry into an unimaginable place where light might shine on and into our bodies' hidden and shameful places and processes.

After the meeting I sat with my friend in her car in front of my house. We talked till late at night, trying to get our heads around the new information, the feeling of discovery and transgression. We couldn't calm down; I didn't want to leave the conversation to go into the house. I didn't want to get into the bed I shared with my long-term boyfriend, who had often agreed with me that something must be wrong with me "down there" because my orgasms were so infrequent and unpredictable.

Soon after, I got actively involved in the feminist women's health movement myself. I became a speaker at meetings like the one at Yale. The high point of those presentations was a live demo: I would take off my pants and undies, lie naked from the waist down on a table, insert a transparent plastic speculum into my vagina, and show a roomful of women I had never met how to do pelvic self-examination using a mirror. The goal was to empower women to examine their own cervixes and see what their vaginas looked like. The most startling thing to most women in the audience was that our vaginas and cervixes are bright pink and shiny, not dark and dirty-looking, as they imagined they would be.

Thinking about it now, in 2016, I don't understand (or remember) why our "feminist women's health" conversations about "health" didn't include much information about orgasms or how to have them. Access to safe birth control and legal abortion was our focus, and somehow the clitoris and orgasm dropped out of the conversation, at least in my experience. The bright light we shone on predicting and controlling fertility and pregnancy penetrated the vagina, but bypassed the clitoris.

It's interesting that we in the second wave thought that if we learned about our bodies, that would be enough to change our experience of sex. Maybe that's because so many of us gave up on the frustrating experiences we had with men, and tried sex with women instead, where it was so much easier for many of us to explore clitorises and orgasms. Or maybe it was because teaching men about our bodies was so challenging and frustrating both mentally and physically. Even a decade later, in the wild world of sexually liberated eighties Manhattan, I still hadn't figured out how to teach the men I dated about orgasm—mine or any other woman's. The relief the women's health movement had brought me from my shame and shyness didn't transfer to being with men.

There was the man I had sex with on his lunch hour who got up and went right back to work the minute he had an orgasm, oblivious to my frustrated and turned-on state. On our next date I made sure to be the first to orgasm, and then immediately jumped out of bed, much to his shock and fury. I took pleasure in explaining that he had done the same thing to me, but it was so routine for him that he didn't even remember doing it. Raw, disturbing ways to "teach" men that my orgasms mattered just as much as theirs. (Maybe that should be a slogan—Women's Orgasms Matter!)

"Sex education, if any, inspired fear in the hearts of the innocent and uneducated in the classroom around me."

"How many people have you slept with?" Can you picture the setting where that question gets asked? I'm seeing cosmopolitans on a high-top Formica table in a dark bar with music playing, girls crowded around the table, cackling with laughter. I've always wanted to be one of those girls. The girl who says, "Ten." Ten is a number that, at twenty-six, I could be proud of. Oh man, I've always dreaded answering this question. Mainly because, unlike in the scenario above, my answer is two. Two men. I'm twenty-six years old, a healthy, attractive, liberal, nonreligious female, and I've only slept with two men in my life. And in the culture I live in, and, more acutely, the city I live in, that feels like an embarrassing admission rather than something that I'd want to get put on a T-shirt to wear around downtown Manhattan or throw up on my Twitter feed. Can you imagine? "I'm basically a virgin, so take THAT everyone #2men #holierthanthou #bowdown #blessed."

Not that there weren't other opportunities. There have been plenty. In college I dated a lot of guys, hooked up with even more. But there was always a panic, always a hesitation, always something that would lock inside my chest and cause me to coyly look up at the blue-balled guy and launch into a list of planned excuses that wound up on a regular rotation by the time I was eighteen. And I've been lucky that I've mostly hooked up with guys who didn't throw a fit, or force me, or guilt me, or make me feel like a prude when I said no. I remember the look on the face of one in particular: I was nineteen, he was a scene partner in my acting class, handsome and strong and really sweet. We had been hooking up on the regular, and at a party on a friend's roof in Williamsburg one night (before Williamsburg was a place you could go to and feel like you were in the East Village) we were kissing sweetly in the dark and he gently asked, and I gently declined. He pressed me, asked why not, said he really liked me, said we'd have fun because we'd been having so much fun (and we did, we really did), and I felt I had to be honest, and the response came out without me being able to control it or edit it at all. When he pressed, "Why not?" I responded, "Because I'm not in love with you. I'm sorry." He looked at me, surprised, smiled, said he understood, kissed me, and walked away. That was the first time I was ever able to articulate the reason why I wasn't racking up significant notches on my bedpost like my friends were. I couldn't sleep with someone I wasn't in love with.

Let me back up and give you a little context. I come from an Italian family. Italian women were supposed to be strong, motherly, well-adjusted goddesses who were to be sexy only to their husbands. This was an unspoken precedent set by my parents. Men were constantly portrayed as the villain in my world: grandmothers warning me about marrying Italian men (my grandmother was chased around her kitchen by her Sicilian husband with a knife, and there's a murky area around some distant male relatives in my family who have been connected to organized crime at one time or another). In my Catholic school upbringing, the priests were regularly being hauled off for questioning (but of course, not to jail) or a different state in a new diocese due to allegations piling up against them, ranging from harassment to full-on molestation or rape.

One of my first escapades in which I attempted to explore my sexuality was when I was in seventh grade and my boyfriend tried to put his hand down my shirt in a cold movie theater in New Jersey while we watched *The Bourne Identity*. I removed his hand and he attempted to replace it, once, twice, three times. And I freaked, a tad overdramatically maybe. I got up, went to the bathroom, called my mom, and begged her to come and get me. I left him there in the blasting air conditioning with a box of Sno-Caps without explaining my hasty departure. According to my mother, we lived in a world in which men were predators, mostly, and at any moment I could be assaulted or raped. (She tried to save me by making sure what I wore wouldn't "get me in trouble.") I spent most of my adolescence watching *Law & Order: SVU* on repeat, which only aggravated my fear, which was rapidly turning into an overall fear of men.

When I signed up to attend high school at an all-girls Catholic school, that didn't help. Sex education, if any, inspired fear in the hearts of the innocent and uneducated in the classroom around me. We watched a recorded version of part of an early-stage abortion in my junior year biology class, and we learned a lot about what would happen to you if you got herpes, or gonorrhea, or AIDS (public shaming, horrifying symptoms that couldn't be hidden, and impending doom resulting in tragic DEATH, surely). We of course didn't learn how one could possibly contract such a disease, or how to protect ourselves from it. Girls who had boyfriends or lost their virginity were slut-shamed by the other girls out of jealousy and fear. Two male teachers at the school were fired: one because he had been tracked and arrested by the FBI and placed on the national registry of child pornographers, and the other because he'd had sex with a student (even though she was of legal consenting age).

In a school run by nuns, mostly bitter, mostly cruel, with crucifixes hanging on at least one wall in every classroom, we were always reminded that God, the *Father*, was watching our every move, so naturally, I respected Him out of fear. At my high school, there were those of us who craved male attention (and would therefore do anything to get it), and then those of us who were scared of it coming from anyone other than our dream boyfriends, our Mr. Rights. Stacking all these things up together, I now have the perspective to realize that I was afraid of boys, and though obsessively "in love" with several over the period of my early youth, couldn't face the idea that one could use one's sexuality in an empowered, healthy way; the way Rachel, Monica, and Phoebe did on *Friends*; the way the fabulous idols of *Sex and the City* so easily did. Sex was posed to me as a crime, a taking of something I'd never be able to get back, and if I was going to pick a sexual candidate and go through all of the trouble of sacrificing that special thing and disappointing God and my family and potentially ruining my squeaky-clean reputation, not to mention the near-guarantee of developing some horrible disease (or even worse, getting pregnant), which would all inevitably end in death—he had better be someone who was worth it.

To further complicate this issue, I lost my virginity when I was sixteen to a boy I was completely in love with, who, at the time, was immature and didn't take our relationship or my feelings seriously. We'll call this boy Sam. I had met him a year before, we fell in love with each other instantly over a short summer, and then he went to college in a far-off place. I was doomed to the fate of that common tale. He quickly hooked up with many girls, came home occasionally, hooked up with me and told me he still loved me, then would go back to school and not pick up the phone when I called. Finally he got in touch and asked if I'd come visit him at school. I obliged excitedly, and on the second day of my visit, he took my virginity in his freshman-year loft bed, his roommate sexiled, Miles Davis playing (Sam was a jazz musician. Duh. Oy.), my face and his back approximately six inches from the ceiling (what other way to lose one's virginity than in an awkwardly executed missionary position?).

The next day, after the emotionally and physically painful affair, we woke up, and he blurted out some excuse for why he had to take me back to the airport six hours early because of one thing or another. He rushed me to get ready, we got in the car, and he dropped me off hurriedly at my terminal, closing the door and taking off without saying goodbye. A few weeks later I found out he had been seeing someone for a few months and things had started picking up just after I left, and that they were now boyfriend and girlfriend. To say I was crushed doesn't even begin to cover what I felt. Not only had I been betrayed by my first love, who had made me feel so special, so beloved over a sweet summer, but even worse: I had committed the crime of giving that sacred, holy thing inside of me to someone who didn't deserve it. I saw all the signs. I ignored them. And there was no way I could get it back.

When I broke out of the all-girls prison of a high school and started college at NYU, I decided to try my best to get over my heartbreak and the fear I had of sexuality. I still loved this boy, but to bury the pain of us not being together and the repeated nature of our affair (the likes of a soap opera), the way I decided to hide my pain and get over it was to hook up with every and pretty much any guy who was interested. Which I definitely followed through on. There were nice guys, egomaniacs, narcissists, and mensches, but no one as worthy as Sam. Date after date, hookup after hookup, I'd flee, claiming I was sick, that I wasn't interested, that I couldn't have sex because I had my period (lame, I know), that I didn't see us going anywhere, and finally, on the roof in Williamsburg, that I wasn't in love. The only person who was worthy, I thought, or at least whom I trusted enough, was someone who had trampled all over my heart. I hated this about myself; I despised the fact I couldn't freely express myself sexually like so many of my friends and childhood television role models, the fact that I feared sex and the connection sex results in with anyone, let alone someone who ultimately didn't mean anything to me. I so longed to share exploits like secrets and tricks I learned like recipes, like so many women my age were doing. But I just couldn't.

I did fall in love a few times with others after that. Early in college, in between my exploits of running away from the sweethearts and the ne'er-do-wells, I met someone. Here was a guy, a toxic infatuation whom I steadily pursued who loved watching me do so and fail. I was willing to forget Sam for this guy, who was just as emotionally abusive, if not more. We fell apart and he left New York and that was that with him. And then there was another. I had gotten into a program in London the year Sam was graduating from college and moving to New York. After a rendezvous where he looked me in the eye and rejected me for the final time, I swore I would go abroad for my first time to just take time for myself. And that's of course when I met someone.

He made me laugh harder than anyone had ever made me laugh before. He was sweet and kind, scared, but a wonderful guy. We had a blast. I don't know what happened with him, or what made me fall: maybe it was because I was so sick of being heartbroken, maybe it was because I was in a new place that didn't remind me of Sam. But I fell happily for this guy, and I remember distinctly the first time we had sex. It was, as all the others were with him, a night of hanging out in one of our dorm rooms, having fun, and laughing until we nearly peed our pants (gals: is there anything sexier than a dude who can make you laugh?). I told him I thought we should sleep together, and he said he didn't think it was a good idea, because he was afraid we'd hurt each other, and because he was getting over a bad back-and-forth relationship. I told him I wasn't afraid, and that, since we'd been having so much fun, it'd just allow us to have more fun if we slept together. And I really believed that. I had fallen for him and I wasn't afraid; I guess I thought that he was definitely worthy of the taking of that sacred whatever-it-is inside me. So we did it. We had sex and it was absolutely, hands-down, fucking life-changing, crazy, crazy sex. And I was right: we had even more fun now that we shared in each other and had amazing sex together.

The minute the program ended, so did we, knowingly, tearfully. I woke up in his bed the morning of our flights and we both cried and cried as we got dressed. We both knew New York wasn't where we could be together, that London provided us the space we both needed away from each of our complicated exes, and though our being together allowed our hearts to mend, New York represented (as it is wont to) getting back to reality. When I landed in New York, I turned on my cell phone and had twenty voicemails from Sam. He was sorry, he wanted to get back together, he needed to see me, he loved me. Some weeks went by where we'd see each other, maybe sleep together, and he'd ask me to get back together and I'd say no. One cold, late night, he asked me to meet him in a diner off 14th Street. I walked in and saw him at a table, hunched over a plate of ketchupy fries, sad. I sat down and he asked me again to be with him and said, "If you say yes, I promise you I will spend the rest of my life trying to make up for what I did to you, and will build something good moving forward. The day I stop doing that is the day you can leave me."

Since that winter, which finally ended a long period of heartbreak, exploration, shame, rejection, and sorrow, I've learned a lot about my sexuality and how intrinsically linked to fear it always was. I'm older now, twenty-six, and last year, when I was twenty-five, in front of my closest friends and family (some of whom had witnessed the grittiest moments of the saga between Sam and I), I married Sam. He's held close to his promise and hasn't stopped trying to this day. Though things were hard between us, and we both caused each other a lot of pain, I forgave so much of what happened, and Sam has proven himself, after all of that, to be *the* worthy recipient of my sexuality, my partner in life.

However, there are still moments when I wish that I had dated and slept around more, or could fabulously dish my "list" to my girlfriends over margaritas, and definitely wish, when I'm around my friends and they talk about dating and sex, that I had experimented more, that I hadn't been so afraid to open up, that I had more notches in my belt. I do wish I'd had more encounters, more experience, more fun. Not to mention that I definitely get spoken to with a lot of well-intended (but nonetheless) eye rolling when I try to contribute my experience or my opinion or try to vent about the problems in my love life. My story of marrying the first person I ever fell in love with somehow immediately disqualifies me from the conversation of singlehood, even though I've been through so much, even though I can relate to every scenario of joy and pain that my friends describe when we talk about love and sex. I get it, yes: the last person you want to have sitting in front of you when you're in pain, when you want to complain about your partner or the unfortunate scenario you're in, is someone who got a "movie ending," believe me I do. But it's almost like I've lost not only membership to the Hookup Culture (was I ever really a part of it in the first place?) but also the right to have problems and talk about them openly with a lot of my girls. There's almost this new culture I've entered; I left behind the Hookup Culture, and am now in the Marriage—in-which-we-don't-talk-about-things-we-used-to-talk-about-because-we're-young-married-ladies-and-we're-wives-now-and-mothers-to-be-and-if-there-are-problems-we-can't-talk-about-them-with-unmarried-people-or-really-anyone-because-they'll-just-judge-us-for-having-gotten-married-in-the-first-place-and-will-then-place-bets-on-when-exactly-it-will-be-that-we'll-get-divorced-if-we-say-anything-so-either-vent-to-your-therapist-or-just-deal-with-it—Culture. Being the married island in the midst of the Hookup Culture is lonely, and that's the reality of it. I don't really fit in. And I don't think I ever did, even when I was an active, card-carrying member. But anyway, I digress. I was talking about my problems.

Sex is still a problem for me. I'm happily married and

enjoying the new life we're creating for ourselves as a unit, because, as a unit, that's how we love each other best. However, just because I **poof** got married, I'm not changed; there's still something about sex that I can't always wrap my mind around being comfortable with, that's still bonded with fear. But Sam and I work through it; we make each other feel safe, desired, and loved. When my husband and I have sex, it's fantastic, and sexy, and deeply loving and emotional and soulful. Sometimes we experiment with a new position, or a book, or a vibe, and wind up laughing about it later if it doesn't work so well. There are times when I'm not in the mood to give myself over, and he knows it, and respects it, and we move on. Our sex is predictable, which, you might be surprised to hear me say, isn't always sexy (coming from someone who typically embraces the predictable). But someone knowing your body that well, that part of you in such a connected way—I can't always give that away, even though it's to someone who deserves it. It's mine. I go through life protecting a lot of parts of myself, and I think My Sex, so to speak, is one of them. And in this world, in this city (New York), where there's so much instability, where change happens and shakes things up, where the feeling of safety, in every sense, feels like a rarity—sometimes I just choose to keep it.

"I hung from him like a decoration, my knees off the mattress slightly as he took my weight fully in his hands."

This Italian/Jewish fellow made me come. For our purposes today, I shall call him Luigi Shmeckel.

I was attracted to his body, but not his personality, though I approved of his ambitious nature. The first thing we both did right to make me come started weeks before with a lot of Facebook messaging back and forth. I was more into him than he was into me, emotionally speaking anyway. When our paths finally crossed, he helped me to indulge in a hit or two of marijuana. I needed guidance because fire, pipes, bongs, coughing, and even matches near my face all freak me out.

The pot proved enormously helpful. I washed it down with half a can of beer, for you scientists out there looking for the perfect orgasm formula.

Due to Luigi Shmeckel's excruciating social anxiety and STD fears, even after discussing recent testing and my entirely negative results, he kept me at arm's length a good while, as my horniness for his sickkkkkk body and my desire to be touched escalated. By the time we were on his shitty mattress sans bed frame in his semi-hoarder bedroom, I was high as a kite. I chose some great music, the band Avan Lava, which I never do during sex, but he was my pot guide and I think he knew how lovely music would be.

Again courtship went slowly. I don't recall much of the kissing or "real" connection. I think it was pretty limited. The music and touch and his body and mine became inseparable and that was incredible. My prefrontal cortex (I'm guessing!) went offline and all stimuli became of equal weight and I was unable to judge myself or him from the outside. Everything was one amazing thing. You know, you've been high before. I hadn't really, not like this.

I was present with and delightfully confused by my sensations, unable to disentangle them from one another.

Then he brusquely said, "Turn over. Put your head down." Now we were doggy style, but with him being six foot three or four and especially long-legged and my body being less than four foot eleven, the shape we made was extraordinarily pleasing to me. I hung from him like a decoration, my knees off the mattress slightly as he took my weight fully in his hands. I was like a droopy half-mast flag, if that were a sensual image. His power and my high-ness were truly all-encompassing. He said again, "Head down. Lower," to get the angle he wanted and the control. His tone of voice was somewhere between robotic and psychopathic. He was just using me as a place to come. I love that feeling. He did, come. I went off to pee feeling pleased enough, with generally low expectations, assuming he'd be selfish.

When I returned, he informed me that now I would come. I laughed doubtfully and felt the familiar shame I feel with men: shame on their behalf at their guilelessness and shame because I'm broken somehow and don't come from...well, men.

I lay back and *what happened next was*...everything. He went down on me, but right away it was different. His endurance never flagged and his confidence was high. I stopped wondering when he'd give up because I began to stop thinking altogether. (Pot was still for sure a key player.) Then he switched to two fingers headed slightly upward, brisk but not painful, light and fast and decisive, and now it felt like he was challenging me, dueling me into orgasm, and I genuinely and quite surprisingly began to lose myself. As usual, as I lost myself, I grew terrified of farting, but I let the thoughts come and then go. He surprised me again, fucking me with three or four thrusts, which I didn't see coming and seems in retrospect to be a signature move. The addition of his cock was super erotic because it reinforced for me his arousal and some of his self-denial at the expense of my pleasure. It also mitigated the guilt I typically feel about taking too long or being a lost cause. I knew he was having a good time because his penis was erect.

Then he switched to cunnilingus again. He alternated tongue, fingers, cock at a thrilling pace that was insistent but never painful, and he switched often enough that he was always just ahead of me. I believe he also threw in a fourth move, which was supersonic clit-finger stimulation. Fast enough to rival a low-battery vibrator and thrown delectably and unpredictably into the mix of his other winning moves.

To my enormous shock and delight, I came as he fingered me.

Then he kissed me lightly just above my belly button, like putting a bow on an expertly wrapped present. He showed me that he knew the event was monumental enough to warrant a flourish. Or, at least, that's the reading I gave it.

Then he set a timer for five minutes to cuddle before parting ways across the shitty mattress to sleep separately. (He has OCD, re: timer.)

I asked him how he did the undoable feat. He said he had read articles and watched videos about it. The bar was raised. Why couldn't other guys do this?

Between his confidence, the homework he did, his endurance, his fitness, his pot, his attractiveness, and my base-level feelings of safety, orgasms were had by all.

Luigi Shmeckel FTW.

"The orgasms I have with him are like nothing I've experienced before."

My two best lovers were the worst and best relationships of my life. The first had a small penis and a bad disposition, both of which he was extremely earnest to overcompensate for in bed. The second has a big penis yet still compensates to the same degree as the first. I married the second. I've had no lack of lovers in my life and my two best lovers are the only two who stand out for giving me orgasms anywhere equal to the ones I give myself. The rest, although some were deep, profound loves, were not memorable lovers. There's something to that.

The first knew how to perform. He was patient and gentle. Although I thought he loved me, love to him was manipulation and control. He was never my friend. I sensed that, and although at the time he was the best lover I'd ever had, he isn't my best lover ever, which in my opinion can be measured by the degree of orgasm. Intention and human connection equal the degree of the orgasm.

I started masturbating when I was around twelve and I feel lucky that I can give myself efficient, satisfying orgasms. But it's a lonely endeavor.

My husband and I lead separate lives. He travels at

least two weeks per month and I too have a demanding profession. In the end, we see each other on average around two weeks each month. Being alone so much, I find it a relief to be able to satisfy myself. It makes me feel powerful and self-sufficient. I get by. I miss him. Then he comes home and we fight until we make love. Sometimes it's hard to make love right away. We have two kids. Our schedules are brutal. We're tired. When we finally get down to it he's my familiar best friend, the sexiest man alive, the person I connect with on every level more than anyone else, ever, in my life. The orgasms I have with him are like nothing I've experienced before. Yes, some are better than others. Sometimes we make love for him and I want him to hurry. Sometimes I give him head and I orgasm, because I want to. Mostly he's intuitive, loving, and giving and bestows upon me the most intense, transcending orgasms I've had, because he wants to.

When I first met him I was afraid, waiting for the other shoe to drop. I had always thought there had to be some kind of a compromise when it came to love and sex—that you couldn't find a best friend who was excellent in bed and was also an open, loving, moral human being. It was too good to be true that I had found the full package in one man. He truly cares about me and he shows me on every level, from the emotional to the physical to the intangible. We just fit so perfectly.

That deep gaze into one another's eyes that feels all at once like you've known each other since the beginning of time, like you belong together, like you see your deepest self in the depths of one another's eyes, is both terrifying and exhilarating. Feeling loved that deeply by someone you love equally and sharing the desire to satisfy each other to your very core, feeling the shared energy of pure love, desire, sex appeal, the fact that he actually really knows when I come, that I'm able to let go and make the weirdest noises I've ever heard myself make yet not feel ashamed. That he makes me make those noises and loves them and helps me transcend my shame and look myself in the eye. That he told me when we met, when I was scared and waiting for that other shoe to drop, that because we fought didn't mean we were going to break up, that our lovemaking would only get better over the years, and to this day, ten years later, he's right, it has: these things are the most pure, beautiful expression of love I've ever experienced. And that's what makes the orgasms he gives me the best orgasms I've ever had.

"He'd managed to make every other girlfriend come. Why couldn't I? What was wrong with me?"

It was summer in New York, so it was hot. We worked together, so it was even hotter. It started out as just a physical thing. We had a playful chemistry. He said that I was addictive. We had sweaty, passionate sex, but I never came. That's just how I am. When he asked what made me come, I couldn't really say. And he made me feel like by age twenty-seven, I should really be able to say. We didn't mean to, but we fell in love.

My boyfriend (BF) was always "uncomfortable" with "my past," which really wasn't much of a past at all. I had just slept with more people than him, which wasn't hard; he was a serial monogamist. I wasn't ashamed of my number, but he seemed to imply I should be. I'd slept with all those people and never came? Did I even like sex?

I did, I do. A lot. Sex is incredibly pleasurable, even when I don't come. But that wasn't enough; he wanted to make me come. And he tried—with his mouth, his hand, a vibrator, my hand. And I can count on that very hand the number of times I succeeded. It was starting to feel less like he wanted to give me pleasure and more like he wanted to win. He wanted to be the one to solve this Rubik's Cube of a vagina.

Now every time we had sex, it was punctuated with a postcoital breakdown of what he did right, wrong, how he could improve. I wasn't his coach, as sexy as that game sounds. I was his girlfriend. I wanted to lie in his arms and bask in the afterglow, not replay the game tape to see where he lost me. Mostly because it felt like it was me who lost. He'd managed to make every other girlfriend come. Why couldn't I? What was wrong with me?

He often made me question what was wrong with me, inside and outside of the bedroom. And four years later, our relationship came to a spectacular finish like I never could. And just like that, I was single.

I wanted to move on, but I wasn't ready to meet anyone new. So I rekindled a thing with someone from my infamous "past." My fuck buddy (FB) is a friend I've hooked up with in fits and starts for years. Just the casual sort of thing BF disapproved of.

FB was sad to see me hurting, but thrilled we were both single for the first time in nearly five years. He couldn't wait to lift my spirits by going down on me. See, he too was on a hero's journey to make me come. But FB seemed to truly derive pleasure from my pleasure. When we finally met up, it was obvious our chemistry hadn't waned. If anything, it'd snowballed. He fingered me in the parking lot before we even got into the bar.

We rushed through two drinks and ended up back in my car. Maybe it was the beer or the pot or the Everest-sized mountain of anticipation, but when he slid his fingers inside me, I got lost. The car fell away. People walking their dogs past disappeared. The street melted. It was like some beautiful sequence out of a Michel Gondry movie. And then, like some beautiful sequence out of a very different kind of movie, I squirted.

The Girl Who Never Comes squirted! And then laughed. Giggled, actually, like a schoolgirl. I had squirted like some thirty-year-old pretending to be a sexy schoolgirl on YouPorn! It felt different from coming. And yes, different from peeing. It felt wild and empowering. Like I was a superhero discovering her power for the first time. I could not stop giggling. "I guess you were glad to see me," he said.

FB didn't care how many people I'd slept with. There was no judgment or pressure. He simply made me feel wanted. BF may have made me the coach, but FB made me the star player. He passed me the ball, but I was the one who ultimately scored.

So many stars need to align for me to come, I never thought I'd be someone who could squirt. But I squirted on FB's couch after a bottle of wine and a joint. I squirted during sex in a NY hotel as the sun rose. I squirted propped up on his kitchen island. And I'm working on harnessing my power without FB. Because I know that with great power comes great responsibility. And I vow that when I do master my power, I will use it for good. For so, so much good.

"Feel free to ask to watch me touch myself. If you haven't already, LEARN TO FIND THIS HOT."

I want you to pay for shit. All night. (At least in the beginning stages. We'll move into partnership and split bills when it's time, but for now, be a MAN. I can fuck a woman if I want, and that's nice, too. But if I'm with you, I'm in the mood for male energy, so please give me that.)

I want you to drive. I want you to be wearing good deodorant, no hippie crystal bullshit. You're a man, your animal scent will break through the product as it is. Just something simple. Old Spice is great. A little cologne is nice, too. Especially if you're a schlubby comedy type of guy who I'd never expect to be wearing fucking fancy cologne. Let yourself be fancy. Be valuable.

Put your hand on the small of my back a couple of times throughout the evening. Make our legs touch or have your hand on my thigh for a little bit. Undress me with your eyes. Visualize making me come. Watch me as I walk to the bathroom. I will feel your eyes on my ass and it will make my clit skip a beat. Find a moment to surprise me with a kiss. An odd, in-between moment, like when we're at the parking meter or something. You couldn't resist. You had to feel my lips against yours even though we were hours from the goodnight kiss that will segue us into bed.

When we finally do get to the kiss that will bring us to bed, we've earned it. We've been charging for hours. Hand on side of face is great, any holding of my head for that matter. Better yet, take one hand and hold me in place by the base of my neck. You're not strangling me, but you're dangerously close. Then MAKE MY BREASTS YOUR BEST FRIENDS. I CAN'T TELL YOU HOW MUCH ATTENTION THEY WANT. I want us making out while naked for a little bit. It feels like we're teenagers learning about all that is erotic. Like, we weren't suuuure we were gonna fuck, we were just kissing and just wanted a little more flesh, then a little more flesh, then... a little... more flesh...

If I initiate going down on you, let me for a liiiittle while or stop me, saying something like "Not yet." Kiss me slowly from the lobes of my ears, to my neck, to my breasts, to my stomach, to my knees, to my inner thighs, then fiiiiinally, after the torture, kiss my wet, waiting pussy. (Note: I don't want you to suck my toes because, well, feet are filthy. I can't get past that. Once a guy just kissed the tops of my feet and I thought that was a creative workaround, but he was holding my dirty feet in his hands to do so, and all I could think was *Now his hands are dirty*.) (Also, yes, this whole kissing-my-body-making-me-beg-for-it thing is cliché, but that's because it's fucking hot and it fucking works and most guys are lazy as fuck and don't do it. Be the guy who does it, and I'll be like, *Damn, this guy is a passionate lover. He's the real deal*. I'll be a little intimidated, which will make me feel vulnerable, which is the same thing as peeling off my panties spiritually/emotionally.)

When you are going down on me, begin by just making out with my pussy. Just lay sweet kisses all over it, then focus on my clit. Be gentle. I repeat, be gentle. Circles with your tongue are great. I hate flicking. I see it in porn all the time and I don't get it. Let your tongue be wide and slightly firm; I HATE that thing when a tongue gets all hard and pointy at the tip. Don't make a dunce cap out of your tongue. Just lay it on my clit and find movement that you can stick with for a while. For me, it's a time game. So prepare to hang out, doing what you're doing for a while. If I say I'm about to come, don't suddenly go faster and harder. Keep doing what you're doing. That's how we got here.

Also, feel free to ask to watch me touch myself. If you haven't already, LEARN TO FIND THIS HOT. You will learn so much about how my particular body works by watching me work with it. This is also HELLA intimate, thus very erotic. AND, let's just be honest—you'll be letting me do some of the work for you. It's not cheating, and it's not diminishing your skills as a lover. It's just me and you investing in the art of orgasm. BUT I'll feel reeeeeally self-conscious if you don't get into it with me (by kissing my earlobes and boobs and whispering sweet nothings in my ear). Anyway, enough said on that. You get it. It's such an easy and useful thing to incorporate into your fucking practice. (Oh, and if you happen to find yourself with a gal who isn't used to this idea, try begging her for it. She might just need to really, really know she's safe to be vulnerable like that.)

Anyhoo, after my pussy gets all this lovely attention… I'm going to reciprocate and you are going to enjoy every second of it. I'm very good at this. I won't bring you to orgasm because I need that dick inside me at this point. I'll be down there maybe half as long as you were down there on me, but that's just because I don't want all this boner time to happen outside of me. (Don't worry, you'll get plenty of head from me in general. If I have a satisfying sex session with you, I'll put your dick on a pedestal. The power of the penis is a VERY REAL thing. He's my hero. I want him to be happy.)

Once you're inside of me, throw in an "Oh my God, you're so beautiful," straight off the bat, especially if I'm on top. Go slow and fast, wing it. Catch the vibe. Be assertive and communicative. Figure out positions by saying things like "Does this feel good for you?"

This is probably a good time to mention that if I haven't had a clitoral orgasm, it's very, very, very unlikely that I will have a G-spot orgasm. The clit orgasm is a gateway for me. So, if you're ever feeling like "Oh, let's be spontaneous and skip some foreplay and I'll just push her panties to the side like Jay-Z talks about on Beyoncé's "Drunk in Love"…you better plan to fuck some, STOP, eat me out (or 69 or do hand stuff), THEN get back inside me so we can BOTH finish. Don't "be spontaneous," then come right away and leave me high and dry while you're in your fucking "refractory period." So rookie. So unsexy.

Oh, while I'm at it, this is also probably a good time to mention my period. If I'm on it, it's not a big deal, we'll just put a towel down. When giving oral, leave the tampon in and focus on the clit. Blood all over your hard dick is punk rock. To be clear, MEN WHO ARE GOOD IN BED DON'T MAKE PERIOD SEX A BIG DEAL. We're all animals. We breathe, we eat, we bleed, we fuck. The more in touch with your primal self you are, the better you are in bed. This subject, in particular, separates the boys from the men. The exquisite lay from the underwhelming shag. The educated, confident male from the ignorant, fearful dude.

Anyway, after we've been enjoying some good ol' sweaty fuckin' for a while, when it's time, you can come on my stomach, boobs, butt, or back. We'll figure it out in the moment. Just ask me. Then just lie next to me and kind of hold me for a minute or two after. A "You're so sexy" would be great here. After that, if we're at your place, get a towel, put warm water on it, and clean me off. It's a pro move and it'll make you come across kind and smooth as fuck.

Hold me as we fall asleep. It's just manly.

I'll spend the night dreaming of your sweet, perfect cock and probably wake you up with a gorgeous blowjob. Mazel tov!

"I can't believe I own a sex toy! I'm such a sexy pervert!"

The closest I've come to coming

Hi everyone, my name is ________, I am thirty-two years old, and I have never had an orgasm. I am now ready to take questions.

"That's kind of old. I had my first orgasm when I was nine."
Technically, that's not a question, but congratulations! Your life sounds fun! And yeah, I guess thirty-two is kinda old to never have experienced an orgasm, but that's my reality so... next question!

"Do you feel bad that you can't come? Like, does it make you feel insecure? Like a failure?"
Yep! Hell yes! And double yes! Next question!

"Have you tried masturbating before?"
Doyyyyyyy.

"But have you tried masturbating with the Rabbit/the Magic Wand/the showerhead?"
I've tried all the tips and tricks, girls. I have never climaxed, but not for lack of trying!

"No offense, but like, what's wrong with you?"
Honestly, I don't know. I get turned on, my pussy gets wet, I get tingly, but I just can't seem to break on through to other side.

"What's the closest you've come to coming?"
Ohhh, fun question. Over the years I've had many passionate, hot experiences, but there's one memory that really sticks out in my mind.

I was a sophomore in college and on a friend's recommendation, I bought my very first vibrator. As soon as I paid for it, I raced home to test my goods. I felt super kinky and dirty. *I can't believe I own a sex toy! I'm such a sexy pervert!* When I walked into the house, my two roommates were hanging out in the living room packing a bowl. "Wanna hit it?" one of them asked.

"I can't. I have homework for my... anatomy class. Yeah, that sounds like a real class. Anyway, I'm gonna be studying hard, so please don't bother me for any reason."

I went upstairs to my room, locked the door, and devised a plan. If I was gonna fuck myself, I was gonna go all out. I didn't have much sexual experience at this time, so most of what I knew about nookie came from rated-R movies. I decided to make my jerk sesh hella cinematic. I turned off the lights, lit some candles, and put on my favorite music, Jeff Buckley's *Grace* (it was the early 2000s).

Then I went into the bathroom and got all slutted up...for myself. I threw on some skimpy black lingerie, teased my hair so it was messy and wild, and put on more black eye makeup than all the Suicide Girls combined. I looked like an underage goth prostitute and I felt HOT.

I got into bed and put a pink rabbit-shaped vibrator on my pussy. With one hand I held the vibrator, and with the other I caressed my body, my thighs, my breasts, my face. Jeff Buckley crooned, "Lover, you should have come over," and it didn't take long for the tingles to start.

Ohhhhh yeah. Uhhhhhhhhh. Fuck yeah.

A warm sensation flooded my body. My mouth was buzzing. My pussy felt heavy and hot.

Suddenly everything was getting VERY INTENSE, like I was being electrocuted, but in a good way. All these parts of my body were sparking. Little fires in my pussy, my knees, my throat.

My temperature was rising and suddenly I felt like I was going to SCREAM MY FUCKING BRAINS OUT. I threw a pillow over my head.

Don't scream, be cool, shhhhh. Keep it together. Your roommates are home!

The sensations were getting more and more intense. I couldn't take it anymore. I opened my mouth, I was gonna let everything out when—

I turned the vibrator off. I couldn't do it. Heart racing, I had to stop. I would have broken the windows with my wild banshee screams.

My body was slick with sweat. I tried to catch my breath. I came back to earth.

And that was it.

I've masturbated many times since. It was never like that again.

"What advice would you give other women who are having climax issues?"

Be kind to yourself. Don't focus so much on climaxing during sexual experiences; try to focus on sensations, what feels good. There are so many things that feel fucking amazing: getting your tits sucked, getting your thighs massaged, getting your clit stroked. Enjoy all of it, don't worry about the result.

Choose generous, loving partners who are patient and warm. Be honest with your sexual partners and let them know where you're at. If they are good guys or girls, they will stick around and explore with you. There can be no intimacy if you're faking it or performing.

And finally, my biggest recommendation would be to research "orgasmic meditation" online. It's an awesome practice that involves getting your clit stroked for fifteen minutes by a partner. There is no pressure to come, it's just an exercise in being present and giving up control. Because your partner is unconcerned with whether you come or not, it frees you up to just lie back and enjoy. It's a great exercise for women who are in their heads during sex.

"Do you think you could be a little less self-critical about not coming and take a more curious and loving attitude toward yourself?"

Yeah, I think that's a really good idea.

"I don't believe I owe my partner a real orgasm any more than I owe her access to my pussy."

Truth? If I decide I want to have an orgasm, I almost always do. From talking to my straight friends, I've inferred that this might be a lesbian privilege—though I've slept with a few men too, and come with every one of them. (The thing for me, with a guy, is to unabashedly rub my clit while being fucked, and if necessary, get him to call me a slut a few times. Done.) Sure, a few times in my life, usually in the context of a long-term partnership, I've tried to come and haven't been able to. But we're talking single digits; if some combination of her hands and my hands and her mouth can't make it happen, my trusty Magic Wand is tucked conveniently under my bed to pinch-hit. A genuine failure to launch is usually due to extreme stress, exhaustion, or problems in the relationship; the rest of my non-orgasmic sex—and there has been a lot of it in the decade since my first time—has been by my own design. Because sometimes, I just decide not to try.

Listen, coming is raw. Coming is primal. Coming is intimate on an epic scale: pearly gloss on a partner's lips, insides pulsing oceanically around fingers or hand. Coming is the innermost circle of my lust and my self, and the criteria for making me come are steeper than for fucking me. There was the dancer with the perfect Hollywood body and the unrelenting moan; the transman whose cock pressed up against me in the bar before we decided to ditch his friends and go to my place; the punky femme whose hands were so small, she could fit one inside me with almost no warm-up. Within ten minutes of foreplay, I decided that each of those people, however hot and lovely, was—at least that night—not going to see me come. I had a good time, and I reveled in the sensory details of fucking and being fucked by them. And then I faked it.

For many years—and like, I suspect, many women—I felt enormous shame about faking. All the magazines (which I now recognize as little more than the Barbie aisle of the patriarchy) told me not to, told me I was ENTITLED TO AN ORGASM, to COMMUNICATE WITH MY PARTNER, and that, most important, faking was a VIOLATION OF HIS (ugh) TRUST!!! While it's well-intentioned (I think?), I can't help but feel that this rhetoric prioritizes my partner's experience of my orgasm over my orgasm. I *know* I'm entitled to one—*Cosmo*'s not wrong there—but I'm also entitled not to have one, not to attempt one, and not to let my partner in on the decision. My faking has almost never been about what my partner couldn't give me; it's been about me managing what I wanted out of sex: the degree of intimacy, the degree of effort, the length of time, my willingness (or lack thereof) to die a little death in the presence of this particular person on this particular occasion. Almost nobody knows how to make another person come right off the bat (not even lesbians), and the dialogue and nonverbal communication that comprises the teaching is sensitive and loaded. In large part, I select partners with whom to build long-term sexual relationships by asking myself, *Who do I want to teach?*

All this is to say: a significant factor in making me come is being egoless about making me come. If it's the first time I'm sleeping with someone, unless sexual lightning strikes, my orgasm might not be real. But neither is my faking it resentful, or resigned, or necessarily a reflection on my partner's performance. It's what I've decided to do with my body in that moment, and it feels right to me, and it certainly does not preclude me coming in the future. I don't believe I owe my partner a real orgasm any more than I owe her access to my pussy. When and if I decide I want to come, I will.

And what makes me want to? Oh, God:

A woman who loves her own body, who lives in it like it's a home she chose herself; a woman who takes her time, who recognizes the power and utility of both tenderness and aggression; a soft, slow, lapping tongue on my clit; two fingers sliding firmly, finally into me; being touched all over; being kissed insanely well; being the bottom in an ardent 69; a woman who delights in the messiness of sex, whose eyes go stormy once I'm naked, who gets a little primal; a woman who is unabashed about her own pleasure, and about her love for other women (and, on the rare occasion that I fuck a man, he's got to *worship* women—like, eat pussy for hours, and do it well). Big hands, tomboyish clothes, confidence, swagger; dreadlocks, curls, blue eyes, brown eyes, tattoos. Strength. Softness. Balance. A particular glance across the room. You know the one. Not the one that says, "I can make you come," but the one that says, "I can make you *want*." The one that stays with you all day, makes you wet, a little rabid. Makes you feel like your own wanting is the whole point, the beginning and the middle and the end.

"Sometimes we try so hard for sex to be casual or animal or merely physical that we forget there can be an emotional underbelly to it all."

How I come when I'm alone

I have a very particular way of masturbating. I like to keep my panties on because it simultaneously provides a layer of protection (the clit is so, so sensitive and this helps me not to overdo it) and if the material is nice, it offers a cool texture to rub up against. There's also the added bonus of getting to see evidence of my pleasure afterward. Seeing my panties all wet post-masturbation is a hot visual for me.

I lie in bed with my knees splayed out to the sides and my toes almost touching so that my legs are in the shape of a diamond.

I cycle through different porn videos. Sometimes I might warm up by looking at erotic still images and then progress to watching an actual video. I feel turned on by a wide variety of things, some of which are intriguing activities I've yet to try and many of which I would NEVER want to do in real life. Mostly because a lot of what I'm watching seems to require CrossFit-level stamina, a high pain threshold, and the understanding that you are never going to have to introduce this person to your parents. Oh, and being unfazed by sticking objects of absolutely any size or shape in your ass. That too.

But porn is a universe where I do not live with the physical pain or the mental discomfort or the emotional repercussions that can sometimes accompany sex in real life. It's sex without context. All turn-on. No thinking about what it all means.

I take the index, middle, and ring finger of my right hand and hold them close together so they're all touching. I rub my clit in small circles, applying gentle pressure (the operative word is *gentle*, not like I'm "out, damned spot"-ing it). Every once in a while, I will switch up the sensation by rubbing up and down, squeezing my labia together, and lighting tapping my clit.

When I'm getting close, I might tilt my pelvis upward and point my toes. Or maybe I'll find myself needing to close my eyes for the last thirty seconds or so. Somehow, those things seem to help get me to an orgasm.

Still, this routine is not foolproof. Sometimes I get right to the edge, but the sensation becomes too intense and I have to stop right before orgasm. When I'm with someone else, it can be somewhat easier to transcend that feeling. It feels akin to working out by yourself versus working out with a trainer. Sometimes I need someone else to push me so I can get that deeper "workout." Speaking of someone else…

How I come when I'm with you

I've never come from straight-up P-in-V sex. It just doesn't happen for me. Sex can feel fucking amazing and I may spend the following week daydreaming nonstop about the next time I get to sit on your dick...but despite this, there will be no orgasm.

I come from a mix of oral and your magical hands.

I like having you lick my pussy; not like you're licking a lollipop, all bland, uniform strokes—rather, treat my pussy like it's my mouth. If you were kissing me, you wouldn't just do the same thing over and over, you'd mix it up. A little tongue here, a little sucking there, a little teasing with your lips. Think of it like you're making out with my vag.

Simultaneously, I want you to be fingering me. I know this may require some multitasking skills, but if you can check Twitter while watching Netflix while eating takeout while talking to your roommate while Gchatting with your mom, you can do this! One or two fingers exploring inside while your mouth is on me is total heaven. Feel free to experiment with what your fingers are doing. When it's good, I will definitely let you know and encourage you.

I also like feeling like you're spreading me open. Incidentally, that should help you get better access to my clit.

After there's been a nice buildup (if the following happens too soon, it's way too intense) and I'm starting to get close, I want you to suck on my clit, keep your fingers inside my pussy, and then stick a finger up my ass. That combination of sensations will make me come so hard.*

My favorite version of this is 69ing. If I get all of the above while sucking your dick, it will be even easier/quicker for me to come.

This is probably because it will help me feel less in my head (after a while of you performing oral, I might start to get panicked you're not enjoying yourself/I won't be able to come for you/your jaw hurts), less detached (when you're all the way down there, my heart and my brain are so physically far away from your heart and your brain that I can feel disconnected), and less distracted (getting to an orgasm can sometimes feel like I'm walking a tightrope; if the slightest thing diverts my attention, I can lose my footing and fall. And once I've fallen, it's almost impossible for me to get back up there).

Also, I love sucking you off, so I will feel extra turned on by this and happy that you get to feel good at the same time!

Miscellaneous relevant information

- Sometimes when I come really intensely, I start crying. It can be an involuntary response, like tearing up when it's cold outside, or it can be

* It's still not a guarantee that I will have an orgasm. I'm not a machine and I can't consistently come like that. Think of that method as a suggestion, a possible place to start from. I want to explore with you. I want us to find new ways to make each other come!

an impassioned therapeutic experience, like I am letting a subterranean emotion out. I think sometimes we try so hard for sex to be casual or animal or merely physical that we forget there can be an emotional underbelly to it all. Please don't be freaked out if I cry. Maybe it's because I am surging with love for you or maybe I've just been stressed out lately or maybe it's nothing...but whatever the reason, know that you have helped me to deeply let go and relax and I am grateful for that.

- If I don't come, it's not as though I had a bad time. At all. If we are having great foreplay/sex/cuddling in the afterglow, then I'm still feeling seriously excited and satisfied. But when you seem to be actively ignoring my pleasure/my vagina, I will feel some permutation of anger, exasperation, rejection, insecurity, sadness...(insert any negative emotion here). I don't want to have sex with someone who makes me feel that way. I don't even want to hang out with someone who makes me feel that way.
- When in doubt, go slow. It can be incredibly sensual and thrilling to let things gradually build up. Yes, sometimes hard and fast is awesome. But I NEED TO BE WARMED UP. The worst feeling is when you're not wet and someone is shoving their dick in you really roughly. This is one of those areas where I feel that porn has done us a disservice. Tend to your lady; make sure she's ready. Two minutes is not foreplay. Yeah, I can make it work in a jam, but it's

not ideal. Take your time before you get to the actual penetration.

- If you're a guy who has never had another guy's dick go inside you, I want you to close your eyes and imagine what it would feel like to have someone else's body part INSIDE of you. Obviously it can feel phenomenal. But when it's handled without finesse, consideration, or taking into account the mechanics and limitations of the human body, it can feel terrible.
- For me, orgasms can sometimes be a little intangible. It's kind of like getting drunk. Yes, sometimes it's undeniable. I can feel that I'm crazy drunk. I can tell that I 100 percent had an orgasm. But there are levels in between for me. There's a "tipsy" level of orgasm, a "three drinks" level, a "you should not get behind the wheel" orgasm. It can be subtle or it can be unquestionable.
- Tell me what you like about my body. A lot of the time, being a woman can make you feel like you are constantly combating unsolicited remarks about your body and feeling sexualized/objectified when you're just trying to go about your day. But that's because it's coming from the wrong people at the wrong time. However, if we're having sex, you are the right person and this is the appropriate time. If I'm walking down the street and someone yells out that they love my ass, of course I am going to feel uncomfortable. But if we're having a great time fooling around

and *you* tell me you love my ass, it will reinforce your desire for me. Feeling wanted by the person I want is just lovely.

- Like I said before, porn exists without my personal context. Real sex, however, is nothing but context. If your sink is piled high with dishes. If you were on your phone the entire night. If you teased me about the sweater I'm wearing. If you waited four days to text me back and I can sense you maybe don't give a shit about me. If your hygiene seems a little subpar—I'm about to have a series of foreign body parts stuck inside me; without even thinking about STDs or HPV or anything, there should be an expectation of, at the very least, basic cleanliness. I'm not saying you have to be addicted to hand sanitizer and have a spotless apartment and always say the right thing and be the absolute perfect gentleman at all times; I'm just saying that all those things are factors. Those things have an impact. They are ingredients in the recipe for me to come. So we could try for an orgasm using your bad attitude and messy bedroom and unwillingness to have a real conversation with me, or we could use higher-quality ingredients like honesty and affection and laughter and comfort, and I assure you we'll have a much better outcome.

"You told me if I didn't act like I was into sex, we'd have to stop dating."

Here are all the times I didn't come:

On the floor of a bathroom in the valley at a true *Clueless* style Val party. You touched me, the first time a boy had ever reached into my underwear. You were so cute. I was wearing a jean miniskirt and a lot of eyeliner. It felt pretty good, but someone started knocking on the door.

In your manual transmission car, parked down the street from my parents' house. Your hand was down my pants rummaging around like you were looking for lost keys in a purse. You were the high school crush of my dreams and I couldn't believe I was in the back of your car. It felt amazing only because I was in high school love with you, not because of the way you were touching me. I never came. I had no idea how to tell you what to do. Even though you asked me to.

In a shitty dorm room, staring at your roommates' bunk bed. You were going down on me—the first person to ever attempt this! I thought, *Finally*, but quickly realized I felt not a thing. I lay there silently like a beached dolphin. You passive-aggressively asked me why I wasn't making any noises. In the moment, I thought, *Noises? What is he talking about?* In retrospect, I think, *LOL, dude*.

You told me if I didn't act like I was into sex, we'd have to stop dating. I laughed and laughed and broke up with you on the spot and rode off into the sunset while flipping you the bird. Nah, I didn't do that. We dated for two more years.

The sex was super fun. You told me if we stayed together over the summer, you'd cheat on me. I was like, ha, what. We broke up. We got back together. I think you did cheat on me somewhere in there. I always went down on you. You never went down on me.

You would finger me and would clearly be so annoyed by how long it was taking. It made me incredibly anxious. Every. Single. Time.

You got visibly bored, so no matter how hard I concentrated, it didn't happen. Body and brain in two different places is not a recipe for orgasm, it turns out.

You made me feel not only bad, but also *ashamed* that it wasn't happening. As if your frustration would make my body be like "Fiiiiiine, we'll come for you, you motherfucker."

When we got back together the third (or was it fourth?) time, you went down on me and actually gave it the old college try. You were awful. A few days later, you got a sore throat, the kind where bacteria grows on your tonsils, and you said out loud at a party, "I think this is from when I went down on you!" as if my vagina was to blame. I was mortified. I didn't say anything. I left the party we were at. I didn't break up with you. I was never breaking up with you.

You fingered me and I finally came!!! It was one of the times when it was a functional orgasm, in that it happened and felt great, but it was definitely not a mind bender. We broke up the next day, because, of course.

We were super drunk. You were screaming at me that you didn't mind if I squirted. I was never going to, because this isn't porn, and I didn't even come close.

You got super frustrated at how long it was taking. I kept assuring you I was close. Eventually you gave up or I got bored or something.

You put a pillow over my head and commanded me to relax. NOPE.

You also got visibly bored, which made me tense in exactly the wrong way.

You also made me feel ashamed that it wasn't happening.

You, and you, and oh, I forgot about that one, also you, made the pretense of foreplay and then we just went straight to the penis-in-vagina part of sex. You came! Good for you! I did not. Discouraged by all other previous attempts in my life, I was straight chillin' like whatever I don't like you anyway this was just a one-time thing.

And then. Let me tell you about the first time I really came.

You were patient and kind. You made me comfortable. Relaxed. Willing to be vulnerable. I fell in love with you. And then, all that made me confident.

I told you exactly what to do.

The second I did, you listened, you followed instructions, and suddenly, on a Saturday afternoon during magic hour, the sunset filtered through wooden blinds, it felt just like that moment in a movie when the camera zooms in on someone's iris, and you see all the ROYGBIV-ness of life in super speed, a crash of sounds, smash cuts to dancing, space travel, people fucking, ending with an opera singer's chandelier-smashing high note.

Now I can come from sex, from you going down on me, from touching, from everything. It's a simultaneous clenching and letting go, with legs spread, or stick straight, or wrapped around you, feeling open and wild and utterly me. I visualize monochromatic color fields, modernist structures and fields, and pyramids, and pleasure, pleasure, oh God, pleasure unending.

"It wasn't until after a decade of promiscuity that I realized what had actually happened."

Ah, the female orgasm. I'm fascinated by it, and grateful to be asked to write about it. In particular, from an evolutionary perspective, is there an essential reason for it? Men must orgasm in order to propagate the species. But the female orgasm seems superfluous—it isn't necessary for conception, and it can happen outside of the context of reproductive sex. So I started doing some research. One theory is that as the female reproductive system has evolved, so has the role of the orgasm, and now it's an unnecessary vestige like the appendix. In some mammals, physical stimulation is necessary for ovulation, and it's possible that human females were once in that category. There is an endocrine surge (including prolactin and oxytocin) in women after they orgasm, and some mammals need this in order to ovulate. In these mammals, the chemicals released during orgasm also help the eggs implant successfully. Human females now ovulate automatically without needing to have orgasms, but maybe this wasn't always the case. Spontaneous ovulation seems to have coincided with a shift of position of the clitoris. The clitoris used to be inside the vagina (what??) and has shifted up, up, and away from it.

Now the clitoris has no reproductive function, and it is the only body part in either gender with the sole function of providing sexual pleasure. Hallefuckinlujah! It only seems fair, considering the many ways in which women get the short end of the stick (pun intended). Did you know that the Equal Rights Amendment was never ratified, and that women are not protected in the Constitution? Go to EqualMeansEqual.com and watch the documentary.

But I digress. When I first discovered masturbation, I was probably around eight years old. I don't remember my exact age, but I do remember that if my mother caught me doing it, she would scold me harshly. She wouldn't say why, but she made it clear that it was bad and wrong. It's tragic that sex has been so demonized in America, often because of conservative religious doctrines. We are taught to have shame about our nude bodies, and any sexual thoughts, desires, or behaviors, unless they're within the context of a heterosexual marriage and for the purpose of procreation. That point of view is the real shame.

My dad had some *Playboy* and *Penthouse* magazines hidden in his bottom dresser drawer, and when my parents weren't home, I used to touch myself while looking at the photos and reading Penthouse Forum. I also found a vibrator in my dad's top dresser drawer, and when I once asked him what it was, he said it was a "massager." I started using the "massager" on my clitoris whenever I was alone in the house. I'm not sure if I ever actually had an orgasm, but it felt really good.

The first time I had sex, I was a freshman in college. I

was sixteen years old because I had skipped two grades. I was at a party, and a handsome senior was flirting with me. He invited me to his dorm room after the party, and I remember that he had a water bed. I must have lost consciousness, because the next thing I remember, I was naked and he was on top of me, thrusting his penis inside me. I was so groggy that I wasn't even sure it was really happening, and by the time I became coherent, he was done. I just thought, *Well, that was stupid. I shouldn't have come to his dorm room.*

It wasn't until after a decade of promiscuity that I realized what had actually happened. I was watching an episode of *Oprah*, and the entire episode was about date rape. *Date rape? What's date rape? I thought rape was when a stranger jumps out of the bushes, beats you up and rapes you, and leaves you on the street, and then you call the police and go to the hospital. So how could that happen with someone you're dating?* A psychologist told Oprah that rape is defined as "sex without your consent," which can absolutely happen when you're on a date. It can happen in the context of marriage. It can happen within any relationship. *Whoa. I didn't give that guy my consent that night—how could I? I wasn't even conscious! So…I was raped? Oh my God.* I sat there in stunned silence. Oprah was interviewing women who had been raped, and she admitted that she herself had been raped. Many of the women who had been raped spoke about their histories of either sexual anorexia or promiscuity, and choosing abusive men for romantic relationships.

It took me a long time and a lot of therapy, but I eventually came to forgive the guy who raped me. I saw him as a little boy who must have been sexually or otherwise abused to grow into an adult who would do something like that to me. The expression "hurt people hurt people" rings true for me. I also had to forgive myself for not knowing better, for trusting him, and for blaming myself afterward. I had to forgive myself for all the years of reckless promiscuity and cruelty to men—I was committing subconscious acts of self-sabotage and revenge.

Of course, the night I lost my virginity, the night I was date-raped, I didn't have an orgasm. I wasn't even awake. I realized while hearing about all the Bill Cosby allegations that I had probably been drugged that night. That handsome college senior must have slipped something in my drink, because what I experienced was far beyond feeling tipsy. I suddenly blacked out, and had no memory of anything until he was penetrating me. As I type this, I feel so much grief. My heart goes out to any woman who has been sexually abused in any way. The common statistic we hear is that one in four women in America has been sexually abused, but in my sphere of female friends and colleagues, it's more like four out of four. Since we are only as sick as our secrets, I hope we all start talking about this more.

Fortunately, my first actual boyfriend after that traumatic experience was kind, loving, patient, and generous. We had been having sex for a couple of weeks when he gently asked me if I was having orgasms. I had no idea, so I told him that I didn't know. He said that probably meant I wasn't, so the next time we had sex, he lovingly encouraged me to let the pleasure build, and when it seemed to reach a peak, to just surrender and let go like I was jumping off a cliff. And that's what I did. It was my first vaginal orgasm, and it was pure magic.

I'm grateful to have experienced many orgasms throughout my lifetime, both clitoral and vaginal, from self-pleasure, from many different men, and indirectly from a few women. It saddens me that I have more than one female friend who has never had an orgasm of any kind, even though my research indicates that it might mean they're just more evolved than I am!

While I still enjoy masturbating and I like clitoral orgasms, they're nothing compared to vaginal orgasms during intercourse. My best vaginal orgasms are wild, epic earth-shattering experiences with aftershocks and tremors that can last for hours. I love making eye contact during orgasms—it intensifies the intimacy of the experience exponentially. I can sometimes be a stereotypical guy after a vaginal orgasm—I just want to go to sleep. But I like falling asleep with our bodies intertwined and with my partner still inside me. And if I wake up because he's gotten an erection again, that's what I call an "alarm cock." Orgasms can truly be blissful, soul-expanding cosmic experiences.

It saddens me that like many women, I've faked orgasms. Why do we do this? Speaking for myself, there have been a number of different reasons. Sometimes it was because the guy's penis was too small or he wasn't good at sex and I knew it was never going to happen, so faking it just helped it be done sooner. Sometimes the guy was good in bed, but I wasn't feeling emotionally open enough to let go, so I faked it. Sometimes the guy was insecure about his body, so I faked it to boost his ego. (There are twelve-step programs for this type of codependent behavior.) Sometimes it began for a specific reason, but then became a habit. Sometimes it was because I wanted to seem super-orgasmic to a new lover, so I would fake more orgasms than I actually had. But all that really did was signal to these men that I was enjoying myself when in fact I was not. I would be horrified to find out that the men in my life were faking orgasms with me. My friend John once told me that he sometimes faked orgasms with his girlfriend. I asked him how that was possible, and he said they use condoms, so if he's tired or not in the mood to exert the effort to continue to have sex, he'll fake it and then pull out. She can't tell the difference, because no semen would have ended up in her vagina anyway. Wow. Let's all stop lying to each other, and communicate what's really going on! I think five minutes of uncomfortable honesty here and there can improve our sex lives, make us feel closer to our lovers, and prevent affairs or breakups down the road.

I wonder if John is the exception to the rule. In fact, it seems like a cosmic joke to me that often during sex, men are trying not to come, and women are trying to come. Men may think about sports or genocide or cement mixers to keep their orgasms at bay, while women may tap into their sexual fantasies to accelerate their orgasms. The holy grail for me is a simultaneous orgasm. When that splendiferous experience occurs with both of us at the same time, it's nirvana. But since a lot of men are built like microwave ovens, and a lot of women are more like Crock-Pots, the chances of simultaneous orgasm can be slim.

I do think at times there is too much focus on the orgasm when it comes to sex—if we're all too goal-oriented, it could take away from enjoying the journey and staying in the present moment. Some men seem to think that once their orgasm happens, the sex session is over. I'd love to explore tantra, but the idea of doing it with a coach or with a group of naked couples in a room feels daunting to me. Maybe I'll start by watching a video about it. In fact, I think I'll go do that right now.

"To put it bluntly, I don't bang dudes who aren't feminists anymore."

My super simple and completely complex guide to getting it on with me

Whether or not someone can make me come starts in the very first moment I meet him. This is true for guys I've hooked up with and for everyone I've dated long term. Because for me, I can't come—*let's be real*, I can't even really get wet—when I don't trust a guy, when I don't feel like he's actually with me, when he isn't someone who can laugh with me when the sound of a queef inevitably happens, or when we both get so tired and realize no one's going to come and we just collapse into a sweaty, breathless, relieved hug. That nebulous feeling of trust, that IT, is why I've come to loooooooooooooooooooooooooooooooove sex. That IT is how I learned to *let* myself orgasm, in whatever loud, messy, shaky way it manifests each time. And I've had IT with new guys just the same as guys I've been with six months or a year or even in a rare, pure, bright spot at the end of a broken relationship. I had it just last week with someone I've only known a few weeks, who I'm falling for, and maybe it will fall apart or fizzle out, but for now, he's making me wet and he's making me come because for the moment, we're CONNECTED (pun intended).

Like many of us, I was raised, however subliminally, to think sex before marriage was okay, but only reeeeally okay if you were in love; like eventually-get-married kind of love. Not real, equal, generous, healthy love, but societally appropriate love. So one day, of course, I did find myself in a sexual relationship for the first time with someone I really did love, who really did love me. But his shame around sex was even deeper than mine. He mostly made me come with just two lazy fingers while he fell asleep and his jizz slowly trickled out of me onto the sheets. For years I felt like a dirty afterthought and a used-up vessel, because I literally was. I came to believe that sex and orgasms maybe just weren't really for me. Why did I put up with that? Why did I believe that? Why am I mentioning this bummer story in this guide to getting it on with me? Because I thought that's all there was, and now that I don't, I *need* you to be someone who understands that *sex isn't a man thing. Or even a man versus woman thing. Sex is a human thing.* To put it bluntly, I don't bang dudes who aren't feminists anymore.

Why not? Because I don't know any women who *haven't* gone through similar things, and that fucking sucks. I'm a teacher, and sometimes I look at the young girls I teach, whispering about crushes at recess and passing notes to boys, and I just hope by the time they really want a dick inside them they've been taught to want it for themselves in a way no woman I know now knew before. We all had to go to therapy and read stacks and stacks of memoirs by wise women like Caitlin Moran or teach ourselves about women's lib in the sixties because they didn't teach it in history class. And in sex ed, teenage boys are taught that they will have wet dreams and that it's okay. Where was that for us girls? I need you, potential sex partner, to see how this is bullshit.

Because I had no idea what it meant to be a sexually alive person, or that being a woman who liked, wanted, fantasized about, experimented with, and just fucking freely had sex when she wanted was indeed very OKAY, I slept with a short string of guys I despised for a while. I thought casual sex had to be with someone I didn't want to be with. I really didn't trust them, but did those dudes technically make me come? Yes. But only through oral. And I'm telling you this, future sex-friend, because it's important for you to know. For some women I know it's the only way (which is okay, of course!), but for me, oral doesn't always count. Even the worst pussy-eating can make me come in just a few minutes if I haven't already come in the last hour. It's truly so easy to do to me that a sandpaper-tongued cat could do it. GROSSED OUT? Good. I hope that means you're getting it.

DISCLAIMER: I'm aware there is a certain kind of male out there who is such a true monster he doesn't even do cunnilingus. I very much believe there can and should be no love without cunnilingus (unless you're two dudes, then you're off the hook). IN THE WORDS OF AMY POEHLER, "IF YOU DON'T EAT PUSSY, KEEP WALKING."

So why doesn't it always count? Because the difference

between oral sex that's *part* of sex *together* and oral sex that's just oral sex *to get the female orgasm out of the way*, or oral sex that's just about how many times a guy can make you come for *his own weird pride*, is the difference between whether or not my vagina and my emotional being are both *actually open* enough to fit a dick in. The amount of times I've allowed my vagina to be rubbed raw after some oral that made me come too quickly before I was even totally wet is WAY TOO MANY. Can we use lube when necessary or just 'cause we feel like it? Of course. But please, please, please don't assume it's the only option. *The more we do this sex thing like it's not just about getting off, the more likely I am to actually get off.* #PARADOX #DEALWITHIT

Vaginas are truly as unique as every painting Georgia O'Keeffe ever painted. If you're not sure you've got a dick that can do the trick or just aren't sure how to take care of me, just communicate. The sexiest thing for me is *talking* about sex with someone I WANT; while it's happening, before it's happening, after it's happened a million times. Because ultimately, that's what it comes down to for me. *Not your technique, but your attitude.* Even in the small sampling of ten dudes I've fucked in my lifetime, I've never been touched, licked, humped, kissed, slapped, bitten, or held the same way. And I'm SO glad. If I wanted to have sex with people from the past, I'd still be with them. I just want it to be WITH the someone I'm WITH right now. Like *in the moment, fully present, sharing an experience* kind of WITH. That may not be it for everyone, but that's it for me.

Should everyone do their best and care about the other

person's pleasure? Duh. Will I sometimes say, "faster/slower/a little to the left"? You better listen. Do I want to be with someone where we can talk about what we want, make requests, try specific new things, and fail at them together sometimes? YES, PLEASE. But I've been in the relationship where "perfect" sex is what he thought could heal broken trust, and it just can't, and I'll never let someone obsess over that with me again. Once the communication stops, my sex drive bottoms out completely and forced orgasms just make me sob. So please, *just talk to me*. Tell me how you feel and what you want. Ask me what I need. In and out of the bedroom.

So to this new guy I'm seeing, or the next new guy after him, or the woman (or wom*en*. I'm open! *Seriously.*) that may come into my sex life, or whatever lovely human out there I hope I get to fuck for life someday, when we get into the bedroom, or shower, or couch, or wherever, please go to town like it's a fucking buffet and you're craving it all and can never get enough, and I promise you, I will do the same. But first, way, way, way before we find ourselves there, look me in the eye, say hello, talk to me like a person, respect my intelligence, be yourself, be vulnerable, be kind, be curious about who I really am, listen to what I have to say, make me laugh a couple dozen-hundred-thousand-million times, and my O'Keeffe will bloom just beautifully for you every time.

A LITTLE TO THE LEFT

"Picture my pussy like a map of Manhattan."

It's Wednesday night, I make it to your apartment without having to scroll through our text history to find the address, and your doorman lets you know that I'm coming up. He remembers me; an unmistakable sign of commitment that is echoed inside my BFFAE group chat as I head for the elevators. I can smell the weed emanating from the cracks of your apartment door.

I'm tingling all over as I wait for you to roll our pre-sex joint. HGTV is on and I know that it's either *Property Brothers* or *Million Dollar Listing* for the rest of the night. We settle in for a smoke, and like clockwork, your hand kicks off the game with an over-the-jeans clit rub. Here's where I should stop you. I should say, "Picture my pussy like a map of Manhattan. If I am lying on my back, Central Park can be a 'landing strip' and Carnegie Hall is my clit. From 57th down to 42nd and between 10th Ave. and Lexington is prime real estate. Times Square is, of course, my asshole. We must speak before we go there." I should also tell you that during this clit-rubbing foreplay of ours, you tend to hang out in the Hudson

River. This is not where the magic happens. This is New Jersey. (New state slogan?) I don't tell you this because I am constantly afraid of creating a reason for you not to like me.

You think you know what makes me orgasm, and this is my fault. I have never given you a reason to think otherwise. I don't want your hand to be sore or for you to think that you're not doing it right. I just can't do that to you. If you actually are interested in what makes me orgasm, just ask. And I don't mean the coy "What do you want to do?" question you drop on me when the only answer we both know you're hoping for is "anal." But if you really want to know how to get me off, just ask.

Or better yet—don't do anything. Keep me at a distance. Be vague when telling me about your weekend plans and never introduce me to your friends. Always be self-satisfied so that I can constantly question my own quality and purpose of life. Have very few personal things in your apartment so that I wonder if you've always been like this or if you have let someone in in the past, and for some reason, I can't be that person. Talk about yourself and your job and your day, but never ask me questions about myself. Let me stay sitting on the couch while I painfully criticize my chipping toenail polish, skin imperfections, and inability to find something funny/smart/trendy/hot to say. Don't ask me about the scars on my arms and legs and don't feign interest in my story. Use my mouth, my lips, my throat for your pleasure and don't worry about taking your time. The small cuts my teeth make on the inside of my upper lip will heal within a couple of days. Don't worry about getting me off. I can put on a good show and pretend you are a sex god because I will always put your ego before my own pleasure. And you can count on that.

"Maybe this is an obvious statement, but sex is just better when it's desired."

Last night I told my boyfriend that something that excites me about sex is illicitness. The first time I had sex was with a Jewish man on Easter Eve and I was making him go to church with me that coming morning because I felt like I had been neglecting my relationship with God for a while. Whoops. That first time didn't end in orgasm for either of us because I pushed him off me, crying about betraying my faith and family and upbringing. After church the next day we came home and had sex again.

I love a one-night stand. I love making out for hours in bars and in doorways and in the street. I love sex on the hood of some rando's car in my own neighborhood. I love staying up all night with unavailable men and giving them too-long hugs and hard kisses on the cheek.

These things do not make me come.

Last night my boyfriend and I had sex in the park in our neighborhood, in the hall outside our apartment, and were on our way to the roof but were foiled by the fire alarm. Sometimes those warnings on doors really mean it. Boy did we have fun.

These things did not make me come.

But they sure were great foreplay.

I came by sitting on his face back in bed in our apartment.

It takes a while. Sometimes I'll masturbate for forty-five minutes before I get anywhere.

It's like a fucking zen mind game—I really have to focus my thoughts otherwise I'll disengage from what is happening to me physically and just go hang my thoughts on errands or song lyrics or things I mean to ask my mom. It's frustrating and unfair because I am not present to the potentially beautiful thing that is happening. But maybe I disengage because it's not beautiful and it's perfunctory and lame and not shared and just not what I want in that moment. Maybe this is an obvious statement, but sex is just better when it's desired. I even find it is possible to coax this desire out of a seemingly dull situation. The key to this is, I think, active listening.

When my boyfriend and I start listening to each other with our bodies, we have some really good conversations. I am not great at communicating in words what I want or don't want, and sometimes I don't even know what that is. But my body sure knows. And when he is asking questions AND listening with his hands and tongue and cock, I am most certainly responding.

I am able to orgasm when I feel this particular combination of excitement and comfort. If I feel at all anxious or disconnected from my partner, like we're going through the motions of sex because that's what you do after going out on Friday night, like picking your nose or putting the dishes away, we're not gonna get anywhere. I'd rather just suck him off if that's what he needs, and hey, I like doing it, it brings me pleasure to bring him pleasure. But my vagina is interested when I feel desired and taken care of. I give in when I know I am being listened to and cared for by my partner, and then I feel like a powerful fertility goddess who can consume and give life to all things and who WILL scream when she reaches the summit, thank you very much, RAAAAWR!!!! It's great.

I think the reason I am turned on by illicit sexual situations is that the container or frame for the moment becomes so clear—we only have so much time (or no time at all) to do this thing or to be together, so the senses become heightened in order to fully experience every little thing.

But this does not make me come.

It's attention, care, listening, and responding of bodies that lay the groundwork for a good orgasm. It's trust and sharing and vulnerability: We're naked! So let's really be naked and worship each other's nakedness! There are lots of tricks and quirks and kinks and fantasies out there, but I think the key to making any of that "work" is to create a safe and intimate space where a person can be exposed and heard and embraced.

"I can't come when I have roommates and I can hear them opening and closing the fridge and talking about which ABC Family movie they're going to hate-watch next."

Things that will not make me come

- I can't come when I'm worried about whether or not I'm being "sexy" during a hookup.
- I can't come when I'm on top and thinking about whether or not he notices that my boobs look weird and long at that angle.
- I can't come when I'm thinking about how girls in porn "orgasm" (light but furious clit rubbing. no jerky motions. only through announcement—"I'm coming, I'm coming, I'mComingI'mCOMINGI'MCOMING I'MCOMING").
- I can't come when I have roommates and I can hear them opening and closing the fridge and talking about which ABC Family movie they're going to hate-watch next.
- I can't come when for whatever fucked-up reason my mind wanders to thinking about death and how I would deal with the inevitable death of the person I'm having sex with.

- I can't come when I'm worried that I might start my period or that my IUD will poke him or that my vagina will in some way do something to embarrass me, like queef.
- I can't come when he's going down on me and I'm worried it's taking too long and I'm trying to do the math on how long the average blowjob takes and whether or not my time to orgasm during oral is fair.
- I can't come when I'm drunk, even though I really, really, really want to.

Things that will make me come

- A vibrator.
- Some good porn where there's no furious clit rubbing and spasmless orgasms.
- Not worrying about being sexy, how my boobs look, or potential period blood, and actually enjoying the fact that I'm having sex with him.

"There was something about Toni Collette, middle-aged and real with a bundle of frustrations and a knee-length khaki skirt, that really spoke to my clit."

I had my first orgasm at the ripe age of twenty-three. I was watching *Little Miss Sunshine* on the couch and there was something about Toni Collette, middle-aged and real with a bundle of frustrations and a knee-length khaki skirt, that really spoke to my clit. (I had to pause the movie and focus on a still of her so that no kid characters wandered into the frame and ruined the wank sesh.) This was an epiphany because up to this point, I had only tried to orgasm internally. I would bang away with my little vibrator, trying this angle and that, faster, slower, deeper...to no avail. I would exhaust partners during sex. I didn't know how to direct them, but goddammit, I'd let 'em try! I eventually decided I was unorgasmable. Until this moment with Toni, I loved sex and masturbation, but I defeatedly accepted that climax just stopped short at a level eight for me.

So there I am, thinking about Toni's character's difficult mom/wife life, sliding my vibrator in and out. Suddenly, it was like a magnetic force guided the quaking pleasure tool out of my drizzly vaj and pressed it to my lonely clit. Honestly, I'd forgotten about her, poor thing. In college, I found the sensation of clitoral stimulation irritating and often urged partners to move past the clit stop and proceed to penetration. Something had changed. I held the shivering vibrator against my clit for the first time and an awesome new feeling began to build. This clit action was nothing like the fumbling college student fingers or wandering tongues that I'd felt before. Yes, Toni, deal with your barrage of problems. It was like an undulating swell of sensation reverberating off my clit and shorting out my breaths. *Oh, God…this is a level nine, isn't it? Oh, fuck. Oh, shit.* I was freaking the fuck out. I'd never gotten this close before. *Am I going to pee? Am I going to burst? Is Toni going to furrow her brow in resentment of her situation?* Level nine and a half blur. There's no more overthinking once you get to pre-orgasm haze. I'm gone in that moment and running purely on sexual instinct. I apply the perfect amount of pressure in the perfect spot (slightly to the right) and the heavens open. Silence and song. Ecstasy and abyss. Absolute orgasmic rapture. Thanks, Toni.

I'm thirty now and I've still never had a vaginal orgasm. Maybe I could, but honestly, I'm not too worried about it. My orgasms are amazing and I have them down to a science. The process is so specific that no partner has mastered it, but that's okay! Good sexual partners are not threatened by this. I love for a partner to be involved in making me orgasm (i.e., nipple sucking, neck kissing, dirty talk, etc.) because they can absolutely improve the orgasmic quality, but it is flourish. Be it hand or vibrator, the coming comes down to me.

1. **I must be laid flat on my back.** Completely flat. No pillows. No significant lumps or dips in the mattress, floor, pile of hay, what-have-you.
2. **My legs must be tightly together.** Even a small amount of leg separation prevents me from achieving orgasm. This rules out having an orgasm during sex. Even in sexual positions where my legs can be together, the proximity of another person's body throws off the angles I need to stimulate my clit in the necessary process.
3. **Hand or vibrator.** Never tongue. Maybe because a person's face impedes the legs-together thing.
4. **Direct clitoral contact is used sparingly and purposefully.** My sweet spot is just to the right of my clit. ("My right, not yours; stop, I'll do it.")
5. **I can't be thinking about or trying to orgasm.** That kills it. Don't ask me if I'm close or tell me to come for you. If I'm alone and I start thinking about how this orgasm will rank or how I need to come already because my dinner guests are waiting, it won't happen.
6. **Once it happens, MOVE THE FUCK AWAY.** For me, there's the moment of achievement, then the life of the orgasm, then the very important aftershocks and cool-down. My body becomes wildly sensitive and I can't be touched. I get uncharacteristically

mean when an orgasm's bloom is interrupted. I'm not proud of that and I'm not a person who gets mean in any other situation. If I'm working my clit while you're kissing my boobs (from the left side, because I can't have you squishing my dominant hand), and my body goes rigid and my head springs back, that means the orgasm is starting. If you don't hastily remove yourself from my person, you will bungle the whole thing. Expect a sharp "Fuck off!" followed by my disappointed whimpering at the loss of an orgasm that never reached its potential. Every stage is paramount. It goes: moment of orgasm, duration of orgasm, waves of aftershocks/mini-orgasms, cool down and catch breath, beautiful beautiful beautiful sleep.

"Each time, without fail, this man has made every single woman he's ever been with orgasm?"

"No woman has ever faked it with me," said Guy I Dated.

That statement sounds super cocky, right? What's worse is that it didn't come from a place of arrogance. It came from a place of genuine oblivion and surprise. And that's the real problem.

In that moment, a few thoughts rushed through my head:

1. Yes, they have.
2. You're a man in your thirties who has spent more than a decade and a half dating. There is no way you've been able to make *every single woman* you've slept with orgasm for real.
3. No way.

Then, I responded:

1. Yes, they have.
2. You're a man in your thirties who has spent more than a decade and a half dating. There is no way

you've been able to make *every single woman* you've slept with orgasm for real.

3. No way.

Then he said, unpretentiously, "I would know if they were faking."

I laughed, but he was totally serious! I told him that wasn't necessarily true, especially if they were good fakers. You don't know you're being conned when you're being conned by a good con artist, am I right?!

This conversation happened after we had just spent the night together and he was unable to make me orgasm through intercourse. He couldn't believe it. I told him a lot of women aren't able to with just plain ol' penetration. We are complicated beings. In my conversations with my girlfriends over the years, most of them were not able to orgasm this way, or found it very difficult to.

On a deeper level, this made me question how we have allowed men to think they can make any woman orgasm every single time. I mean, women are complex, in the head and in the vaginal area. It takes time to learn the woman, what she likes, and what makes her come. And it ain't that easy. It's not just penis in hole, back and forth, and then BAM, BIG O! I'm not saying 100 percent of the women this man has been with were faking it, but just percentage-wise it feels a little impossible that 100 percent genuinely orgasmed so easily! Each time, without fail, this man has made every single woman he's ever been with orgasm? Through sex? I mean, really. That's too good to be true!

This then made me think about why women fake it. There are a number of reasons, I suppose:

1. We want to be nice.
2. We don't want them to feel bad.
3. *IF* they are working hard to get us to come, we want to give them the satisfaction of thinking they've actually made us come...even if they haven't...so they don't feel bad.
4. It's taking too long and he's not getting it, so we just want it to be over with.

You know those parents who let their children be dicks because it's too much trouble to correct them and tell them not to be dicks, so then you just end up with a kid who turns into an adult who's a dick? That is what happens when women fake it (for whatever reason) and do not communicate to men honestly about how to make them orgasm—you end up with a grown man, Guy I Dated, who truly thinks that he's made every woman he's ever been with orgasm just by sticking his penis in her! They need to know it takes work and that every woman is different! We must stop this vicious cycle!

I dated this guy for a while and never faked it. Eventually, through verbal and nonverbal communication, he figured out how to make *me* orgasm, and, in the end, he could proudly walk away still thinking, *No woman has ever faked it with me*. ;)

"My pussy is your spirit animal."

What I know to be true about getting me off:

1. You need to look at/think about/feel my pussy like it is a luxury oasis spot and it's been years since you've seen something so beautiful, like you cannot wait to rub your face all over that Fiji water spring.
2. You need to be patient. You have all the time in the world and your favorite hobby is watching her (my pussy) get wet and react to your flicks, sucks, and pokes. She cannot sense any moment of boredom, tiredness, or frustration.
3. Audio: We (my pussy and I) want to hear you moan with pleasure at the fortuitous moment we have bestowed upon you. Voice your gratitude and enjoyment for the task at hand, and reassure me that you wish this could be your career.
4. My pussy is your spirit animal.
5. Take breaks from fucking me to go back down because you just have to taste me again.
6. Compliment us.
7. Balance the dichotomy between getting to know my

clit—slowly becoming familiar, exploring me from different angles, opening me like a present—and simultaneously being its oldest friend—confidently taking charge, commanding, and anticipating the familiar reactions.

8. Once in a while let's take turns having selfish sex where the only objective is getting me off.
9. Dan Savage put it best: the ability to make a woman come starts with foreplay, which actually starts as soon as the last orgasm ends.
10. And maybe it's the middle child in me, but feel free to say my pussy is your favorite.

"It seemed a problem of epic proportions and I hoped the feminist movement would address it somehow."

One afternoon in 1955, I came home from first grade and found a children's book entitled *The Wonderful Story of How You Were Born* on an end table in the living room. I immediately read it and showed it to my mother. "Is this true?" I asked. In response to my two other questions, she assured me that sexual intercourse didn't have to take long, and my future husband and I could keep our shirts on. I loved babies and concluded that this was a small price to pay to get one.

About four years later I discovered that I could have an orgasm from contact with a pillow through my pajamas. The feeling included almost all of my body and seemed like a delightfully private thing to do. I didn't think it had anything to do with sex but that it was one of the magical benefits of nature, like fireflies and rainbows.

Some months later I learned that my wonderful feeling was officially called orgasm and was, in fact, related to sex. I came upon this intel by reading descriptions of various kinds of sexual activities in anthropology books that were stored in broad daylight in bookcases in my family's living room. Sex, babies, orgasm—it kind of all made sense to me.

However, when the main alpha girl in my class huddled a bunch of us together during fifth grade recess to tell us that she *found out what men and women do when they want to have a baby ugh can you believe it?!*, and the other girls reacted in similar horror, I kept my perspective to myself. Fortunately I had learned from those anthropology books that despite my apparent difference from my friends, I was on track for a healthy sexual relationship. I concluded that as long as I kept my orgasm experiences to myself until I married the father of my future children, I'd be acceptable to my friends.

A couple of years later, when I kissed a boy for the first time, I felt a new kind of intense and pleasurable feeling throughout my body. I felt less socially deviant about this experience and mentioned it to my friends. Blank stares all around.

As I maneuvered my way through adolescence, there were issues related to being female that were more confounding to me than orgasm. I had to avoid being "too smart" in school if I wanted to have a boyfriend. I had to deny interest in sex so I wouldn't get "a reputation." I had to wear high heels and sleep with scratchy rollers in my hair so I could be "attractive," which was code for being "appropriate," which was code for "guys rule." Etc., etc., etc.

One day in high school I was let in on another *ugh can you believe it* piece of information: the prettiest girl in eleventh grade was a *slut* because she gave the wealthiest boy in twelfth grade a *blowjob* in his red convertible in a supermarket parking lot, no less. Oh, now I'm supposed to condemn her? I already felt sorry for her for not having her genital area involved in the activity in the car, but I was too intimidated by the status quo to defend her.

I entered college as some social mores changed, thank goodness. I had sexual intercourse with my boyfriend, and found that orgasms from vaginal penetration could be more intense than the kind I had already experienced. My younger sister remembers asking me around that time what an orgasm felt like, and my telling her that it was similar to hearing a favorite song. Samuel Barber's *Adagio for Strings* was one I had in mind.

Some months later I participated in my first women's consciousness-raising meeting, which took place in a dorm room. The topic was "The Myth of the Vaginal Orgasm," based on the recently published article of the same name by Anne Koedt. All around me girls were saying, *Yeah, it's a myth all right... uh, what's an orgasm?* I surreptitiously scanned the faces in the room to gauge consensus on this one. I was in the silent minority again.

The week before, my boyfriend had suggested we try *this thing called cunnilingus*, and I thought, *Good for him.* Maybe his parents had the same books lying around their house. Unfortunately, it was not good for me. It seemed pretty much the same as his rummaging around in his desk drawer searching for an eraser. I thought that if oral sex was the dominant route to orgasm, no wonder so many women didn't know what an orgasm was. It seemed a problem of epic proportions and I hoped the feminist movement would address it somehow. I was so optimistic in those days, even though I was still trying to recover from being asked to get coffee for the guys running the Students for a Democratic Society meeting.

Years later, due to a combination of a predictable menstrual cycle and frequent business travel, my husband and I were able to know exactly when our child was conceived… my greatest orgasm ever.

"And while there's something encouraging about the *NEVER GIVE UP!* set, the fact that mostly they blow past the fact that I tell them it's not going to happen kind of cancels out their good intentions."

How to make me come? You won't—but it's okay.

Let me be clear: I really enjoy sex. And I really enjoy orgasms. But I've just never had another person bring me to orgasm. And not for lack of trying—I've had some very patient, lovely, giving partners who gave it their best effort, but it just doesn't happen.

To get these things out of the way: I can and do come from masturbating. I'm quite flexible in that regard—I can get the job done in under a minute, start to finish, if I want to, or play around and take a while, even climax multiple times. I can use a vibrator or toys that insert, or I've done it with neither and just the right kind of pressure. I've tried masturbating more, less, abstaining completely. Using toys during sex. Sex with women. Sex with men. Both at once. Vaginal. Oral. Anal. Any combination of the three. Relaxation techniques. Meditation. Sex therapy. Etc., etc., ETC. Nutshell: if you just had a knee-jerk reaction of "Oh, maybe if you tried..."—I've tried it.

So now, one of the biggest decisions for me, when it comes to sexy sexy time, is when do I divulge this little tidbit? Because I'm not trying to say that I'm giving up and throwing in the towel—using all caps to proclaim, "I WILL NEVER COME FROM SEX." It very well may happen at some point, me coming from the actions of another human. But considering the pretty sizable number of people I've tried with, and the imaginative range of different sorts of "solutions" I/we have tried, I'm just pretty sure right now it's safe to say that it probably won't happen.

So, imagine with me, if you will, that you've connected with a man (in this scenario, you are a woman who mostly sleeps with men), and you two are going to have sex. Say you're in the bedroom and clothes are coming off. When would you tell him? When would you mention, "Oh, by the way, I'm probably not going to come." Don't rack your brain—there's no right answer. Bring it up before the fact and most often they get the little "I'm going to be THE ONE to MAKE. THIS. HAPPEN!!" gleam in their eyes (or actually proclaim it to you—which has happened on more than one occasion), which is pressure that no one needs in this situation. If I don't mention it at all, responses run the gamut: I get the men who say, "I can't wait to make you come again" (...Pardon? *Again?* How quaint.), the men who don't notice—they come and it's done and a nonissue to them (the majority of men I've slept with), and then the ones who just keep going, refusing to be done until I come (bless their dear, sweet, enthusiastic little hearts). And while there's something encouraging about the *NEVER*

GIVE UP! set, the fact that mostly they blow past the fact that I tell them it's not going to happen kind of cancels out their good intentions. Mostly I won't mention it at first as a way of sussing them out. If he's one of the "I'm done and don't care" kind of fellas, it doesn't matter one way or the other—he won't have a repeat performance. I used to think that telling them up front would alleviate the pressure, that then we could let that go and just have a good time otherwise, but it actually had the opposite effect. So usually, after we've been enjoying ourselves for a bit, or if they bring it up (two thumbs up for them if they bring it up before I have to), I'll say something along the lines of "I'm not going to come, it's not going to happen for me tonight. I'm enjoying myself, don't worry, but just so you know." And then, if it's going to be a regular thing, I'll open up and have the whole chat about what the deal is.

I would really like to come during sex. I've been able to incorporate my particular way of masturbating into sexual encounters with two separate men. It involves (generally) a vibrator, a pillow, and me on my tummy on the edge of the bed to get pressure in the right direction. It's not subtle. I'm embarrassed that that's what it takes. Not in the privacy of my own home, but when I first share what I have to do with another person, I'm kind of a swirly vortex of shame and "This is weird and I'm defective." Even though I can consciously acknowledge this fact, I find I'm still pretty much helpless to that feeling in the moment. I've had many, many partners and only been able to climax while masturbating while they're around with two of them. I've tried with a handful more and it wouldn't work. With most I haven't even brought it to the table. I'm sensitive, and my shame around this runs deep. With those two where it did work, and in fact was incorporated regularly into our sex, we'd fool around for a bit, then I would masturbate while he would touch me (gently and on the face or shoulders), maybe kiss me softly, or not touch me at all—maybe just sit back and touch himself. And then, we'd come back together for the intercourse portion of the program and he'd usually get off then. And it's great. It feels like we both have our needs met and that my experience matters—in a way that is conscious of and understanding of the nonphysical ingredients.

So I guess, if you really want to know how to make me come, the answer would be: Do your best to make me feel comfortable with you and be communicative. Don't put pressure on me about it. Ask questions—if I have come yet, if there's anything I would like you to do, etc. Be patient. Believe me if I say it's not going to happen tonight. Make sure that you want me to come because it's something wonderful that you wish for me, not because it'll make you feel like the hero in a romance story. Hang in there with me. Know that the physical part with you is fun and feels great and makes me smile like a crazy person afterward whether or not I come, but feeling safe and open and knowing that you are on the same page as me is what will let me open up about what I need and ultimately achieve orgasm.

"I had HEARD about this clit thing, but I was like, no way, I don't have that, or if I do it's definitely broken."

How I learned to orgasm

I'm turning twenty-nine in four days.

I've had sex with ten people.

Only one has made me orgasm.

The first guy I was with in my freshman dorm room couldn't hide his bafflement when I didn't "make noise" during sex.

And I was like, "Are you supposed to make noise?"

He said, "I don't know, I guess so?"

So, like any good student, I tried it. And making noise WAS a good way to get someone to care about what I was feeling…and I actually used it to get most guys to think that they were achieving something. I convinced a lot of people that I was feeling things I wasn't, and I went through this chunk of my life not understanding my body enough to know that orgasm was a possibility for me. I thought I was one of those girls who just couldn't do it. But eventually I watched enough TV and overheard enough conversation to catch on to the fact that I was stuck under a rock…

I come from a small town in New England—where you don't learn about sex or talk about sex and by default you know nothing about sex. And when I moved to New York City, I was so overloaded with every type of sensory stimulus that my brain kind of exploded. And by sophomore year, and my fourth sexual partner, I knew that I hadn't experienced sex the right way. I heard somewhere that every woman should learn as much as she possibly can about her body before she lets someone else all up in there. Good point. So I grabbed one of those mirrors that come with the blush at CVS, and one afternoon when my roommate was out, I took a long, taxing look at my vagina. I touched it, trying to find my clit, because I had HEARD about this clit thing, but I was like, no way, I don't have that, or if I do it's definitely broken. But what ended up happening is that I taught myself everything no one was going to teach me. And after I found my clit (holy shit) I waltzed into this beautiful sex toy shop called Babeland and I bought myself the most generic-looking and -operating dildo and I practiced how to orgasm from the inside (holy shit). And when it ran out of C batteries, I replaced them. I was basically keeping the bodega in business with my battery purchases alone. And I practiced until I got so good and so orgasmy that I began to notice some other really important issues I had with sex. Mainly this issue of confidence. Because when you're lying in bed alone, fondling your newly discovered vagina, rather than lying in bed with a partner, EVERYTHING CHANGES. Fuck.

So it turns out that just because I discovered enough about my body to achieve orgasm while seated over the engine on a bus listening to Justin Timberlake, it didn't mean that I knew how to let someone else discover that. So I decided, as I do with many things in my life, to become the BEST at giving sex. I was overcompensating for my lack of sexual self-confidence with this Kanye-inspired "I'm a sex god" mentality. I didn't know that being good at sex didn't mean pleasuring your partner to the ends of the earth. It actually meant being pleasured too, and I felt miserable that I couldn't do that because of NERVES. The epically insecure corners of my soul didn't let new guys see me naked, and they couldn't make me orgasm no matter how hard I, or they, tried. And I spent many a night consoling guys who felt bad that they came so early, while being secretly ecstatic that the encounter was over.

Then one night—as this story ends with one single orgasm—someone decided that if I wasn't turned on, he wasn't turned on. And that exploded my brain yet again. And as I'm still picking up the pieces from the cracks in the floor, I can tell you that the best sexual experiences I've had happened when I was guided into pleasure and made to feel comfortable by someone not stopping until he figured out what worked for me. I was asked if what he was doing felt right. He told me what to do for him. He called me out when I was lying. And while at first that type of guidance seems like HOLY SHIT I DEFINITELY GRADUATED FROM THE NEW YORK CITY SEX SCHOOL AND I'M STILL BAD AT THIS??—it's not that. It's that you're responsible for another human's pleasure and that is one of the hardest things to master.

And herein lies my thesis: Once you discover what works for you, you MUST then go teach it to your partners. Practice what to say, just like you practice how you look, how you act, or how you breathe in a yoga class. When the time comes to put your pleasure into words, you're going to have to be kind to yourself and to your partner. Because being the only sex god in the room is a lonely existence.

"Tell her she tastes amazing right off the bat."

How to make HER come

The only thing that feels better than coming is making a woman who has never come come. Take it from me, a real live lesbian! Let's travel back in time...

[Time-travel sound effect]

Welcome to the year 2002. The number one song is "Hot in Herre" and the president is Bush. Little does thirteen-year-old me know that things are about to get *hot* in *my* bush! And if you're not a fan of wordplay, you probably shouldn't read on, I fucking love puns.

When I was thirteen, I literally dared myself to masturbate. I had read about the female orgasm in a book my parents gave me (thanks, guys!) and thought it sounded like an absolute blast, so, one fateful evening, I pinkie-promised with my two pinkies that I'd give myself one.

I knew I needed some sound going on in my room to allay parental suspicion, so I popped in the only movie lying around, *Airplane!*, and set to touchin'. I didn't really know where anything was, y'know, *down there*, but at around the point when passengers started birthing eggs from their mouths, I reached that crucial moment I now refer to as "I'm close!"

The thing is, at thirteen, "I'm close!" felt more like "I'm unfamiliar!" so I stopped the repetitive circular motion cold. Also my middle finger was downright exhausted. Then I remembered my solemn dare. Just like Ted Striker had to steel himself to land that crazy airplane in spite of the unknown, I too had to recommit to my mission. So I buckled down, pushed past the point of no return, and totally friggin' came!

From that moment on, masturbating was my anti-drug. And it all started with a D.A.R.E.

Part of my justification for nonstop 'bating was that it wasn't just for me. A burgeoning lesbian, I felt that it was excellent practice for the vaginas in my future. Speaking of the future, let's cut back to the present.

[Time-travel sound effect]

Welcome back to today. The number one song is probably Drake and the president is definitely trash. But I have some wisdom to disseminate.

No two vaginas are alike. (Maybe twins? Better ask the guys from those Coors Light "And twiiiiiins!" commercials.) You essentially become a thirteen-year-old again when you encounter a new vagina; you *sort of* know where everything is, and you *sort of* know what to do, but you don't exactly know how to please her.

And sometimes, she doesn't yet know how to please herself. Now, I'm no lesbian lotharia, but I've been lucky enough to bump uglies with every number on the Kinsey scale *and* give a couple of women their very first orgasm. What's astonishing is that whether a woman was a chronic masturbator like me or has never even taken a handheld mirror to her vagina, I've found our two biggest hang-ups regarding the Big O are typically the same: *time* and *taste*.

"Am I taking too long?"

"Do I taste okay?"

That's where communication comes in. (Unbelievably hard not to write "cum-unication" or "cums in.")

My advice to all you givers out there is to not give her time to ask about her taste. Tell her she tastes amazing right off the bat. Tell her you have all the time in the world. Tell her you're exactly where you want to be. She can take an *Airplane!*-length amount of time to come and you'll love every second of it and ice your jaw tomorrow.

And to all you receivers, a little overencouragement is fine, but faking it teaches bad habits. (We've all been there! I'm coming right now! ;) .) Learn what makes you come, and tell your giver.

Also, and this is true, everything tastes the same after four licks.

The Afterglow

In a strange kind of serendipity, days before this project went live online, after months of reading women's deepest sexual thoughts daily, I met someone. Someone I fell in love with. Hopefully, the takeaway from that isn't "Read a bunch of essays on orgasm and then get a cool boyfriend!" Because if I could deliver on that kind of promise, I would be getting a million-dollar deal on *Shark Tank* right now. (Is being on *Shark Tank* everyone's collective fantasy now? Is that slightly destructive? Is this my new book idea?)

But despite there not being a true causal connection between working on this project and starting a relationship, it doesn't feel like a total coincidence that after a period of deeply engaging in nonjudgmental compassion and enthusiasm for other women's ideas about sex and love, I once again found myself in a place of feeling positive and curious and accepting.

But this time, with more information. I was no longer seeing sex through rose-colored glasses; I was simply seeing. And seeing things more clearly forced me to learn and process things on a personal and global scale that may otherwise have gone unacknowledged.

I know that being in a relationship or creating this book doesn't mean that I'm suddenly an expert on my own sexuality (or anyone else's) or that any issues I may have are now solved, but it feels good to know that a deep investigation into women's sex lives allowed for a deep examination of myself.

When I read these essays, I didn't expect to feel so affected. To be sobbing at the dining table/counter space/desk in my little studio apartment. To be cracking up as I saw something I'd experienced explained perfectly by someone else who'd gone through the same thing. To be impressed and surprised and turned on and hopeful and anxious and concerned and excited and invested—it was super powerful for me.

Many women told me they were surprised by how difficult it was to write their essay, but ultimately how therapeutic it was. Now that you've read this book, I invite you to unpack your own sex life and write your own "How to Make Me Come" essay, whether it's solely in your head or ends up on paper.

A lot of people have told me that since writing or reading these essays, they had super-honest conversations with sexual partners in which both people revealed previously unspoken thoughts. This is *huge*, people!

I wish for you to have conversations with your partners that are both honest and kind. I want you to be receptive and understanding of the experiences and details that your partners share with you. This is a tall order, I understand. It is not easy to say precisely what you mean at exactly the right moment in a manner that is both eloquent and completely understanding of the needs of your audience. I mean, it can be hard enough to figure out the best moment to tell someone they have something in their teeth, let alone when to tell someone you need a little more suction action on the clit. But it's worth a try.

I'm still learning. Not only how to get better at having these sorts of vulnerable discussions in my personal life, but also how to explore the larger discussions that emerge from these essays. This book has a finite number of pieces, but I'm hoping to hear of more experiences and to continue this ever-expanding conversation. Do you want to be part of it? This is just the beginning.

Acknowledgments

From the depths of my being, my sincerest thanks to:

All of the women who contributed to this project. It quite literally would not exist without your brave, beautiful, candid writing. Thank you for trusting me and being so open. You have left an indelible imprint on my heart and I am forever grateful.

Everyone who supported the *How to Make Me Come* Tumblr. Thank you for reading it, writing about it, and spreading the word.

Emily Greene, who told me, "You *have to* write about this," after I waxed philosophic about orgasm over breakfast tacos. From the bench on East 7th Street until now, thank you for always urging me to follow my artistic instincts.

Jen Ruiz, Andria Kozica, Katherine Mills, and Scarlett Bermingham for your sweet photography and Photoshop skills. Also to everyone who generously lent their homes and selves for *HTMMC/Moan* imagery.

The incredible and inspiring Rachel Bloom, for taking the time to write a funny, wonderful foreword.

Hannah Brown Gordon for your encouragement and smart, kind feedback. Thanks for helping me usher this book dream into reality.

Yfat Reiss Gendell for joining this project with so much energy and excitement.

Thank you to everyone at Grand Central Publishing for believing in this project. In particular, Libby Burton and Maddie Caldwell, for your insight, thoughtfulness, and senses of humor.

Britton Rizzio, Noah Rosen, and Greg Shephard for cheering me on enthusiastically.

My loving friends from GRHS to ETW to LA (with extra hugs towards Emily, Kat, Leah, Lindsay, and Allison) for calming down my persistent anxiety throughout the tumultuous creative process. I truly adore you.

Anthony, who stayed up til five a.m. with me the night before the launch of *HTMMC*, helping me check for typos and keeping spirits high. You have been supporting me and boosting morale ever since. I love you.

Mom, Dad, and Ezra. I am so lucky to have you. Thank you for your constant love and support. I love you!